GLOBAL PURCHASING

HOW TO BUY GOODS AND SERVICES IN FOREIGN MARKETS

GLOBAL PURCHASING
HOW TO BUY GOODS AND SERVICES IN FOREIGN MARKETS

Thomas K. Hickman
William M. Hickman, Jr.

BUSINESS ONE IRWIN
Homewood, Illinois 60430

© RICHARD D. IRWIN, INC., 1992

This publication is designed to provide accurate and
authoritative information in regard to the subject matter
covered. It is sold with the understanding that neither the
authors nor the publisher is engaged in rendering legal, accounting,
or other professional service. If legal advice or other expert
assistance is required, the services of a competent professional
should be sought.

*From a Declaration of Principles jointly adopted by a Committee
of the American Bar Association and a Committee of Publishers.*

Sponsoring editor: Jeffrey A. Krames
Project editor: Gladys True
Production manager: Diane Palmer
Designer: Heidi J. Baughman
Compositor: Impressions, a Division of Edwards Brothers, Inc.
Typeface: 11/13 Palatino
Printer: Arcata Graphics/Kingsport

Library of Congress Cataloging-in-Publication Data

Hickman, Thomas K.
  Global purchasing : how to buy goods and services in foreign markets /
Thomas K. Hickman, William M. Hickman, Jr.
     p.   cm.
  Includes bibliographical references.
  ISBN 1-55623-416-3
  1. Purchasing. 2. Industrial procurement. 3. International trade.
I. Hickman, William M.   II. Title.
HF5437.H53 1992
658.7'2—dc20   91-34449

Printed in the United States of America
1 2 3 4 5 6 7 8 9 0 AGK 8 7 6 5 4 3 2

*To my parents, my wife, and all the other teachers who contributed
to what went into this book.—TKH*

*To all those, especially Judy, who believed more firmly than I
that it would get finished.—WMH, Jr.*

PREFACE

Some years ago Bill called me to ask if I knew of a book that he could use to teach about buying overseas. I knew of none but suggested several that touched on the subject. There are books on doing business with almost any country; books on banking include in-depth treatises on letters of credit and bank drafts; the Department of Commerce tome on commodity controls is huge; and many other volumes speculate on economic conditions, now and in the future, all around the world. Together, we could find none that simply addressed buying overseas. I offered to help him develop a syllabus that could be used for the class. He declined, saying that sounded like more work than he had in mind to prepare for the semester.

During the search, Bill called several publishers to ask if they had any books on the subject. No, we don't, was the unanimous response. One, Business One Irwin, said, "No, but would you like to write one?" The result has been far more work than the syllabus would have required.

This book is for people who know they can get a better, more reliable, or less expensive product than they are getting now. They may not be able to get it offshore, but this book will at least tell them how to find that out, and if it is possible, how to go about it. It is directed at buyers who are not currently buying products or services offshore but who are, nevertheless, expected to find goods and services at increasingly lower prices and higher quality.

It is aimed specifically at the beginner in doing business offshore, but not necessarily at the beginner in business. It does presume some exposure to purchasing in that it treats the business of buying overseas by contrasting it with purchasing domestically. Further, we hasten to stress that it does not aim to teach the full scope of purchasing offshore. It attempts to explain the rudiments of each of the steps necessary to buying offshore, making a complete transaction possible, but does not cover any of them in the depth a single book on each step would.

It explores possible areas of opportunity for offshore procurement in the next decade, focusing on the most likely countries and regions, but virtually ignores areas where civil unrest or economic conditions offer little chance for the inexperienced buyer to be successful. It outlines some ways buyers new to doing business offshore can overcome their lack of personal and business contacts, the real hallmark and asset of buyers who are successful in purchasing overseas. It addresses the impact of culture on doing business offshore and explores how the process of negotiation may be affected by other cultures. It also examines the requirements and mechanics of actually implementing the importation of goods, the unavoidable issues of shipping, customs, and making payment internationally. Last, it provides some suggestions on managing the distant relationship between the U.S. buyer and an offshore supplier.

The attempt to explain the steps necessary to complete an overseas purchase in a single volume has led to an additional focus—the many risks of buying overseas. Although it may not describe the most efficient or cost-effective means of procuring any given commodity, it does identify where most of the risks lie and tries to explain how to avoid them. Although this book may not make an instant success of the buyer trying to make a purchase offshore, we know that it will be a guide in how to avoid instant failure.

A broad understanding of some of the global pressures on sourcing will be needed to make the strategic decisions of an overseas procurement program. In Chapter 1, Buying in the Coming Global Economy, we have identified the salient characteristics of the successful exporting countries and identify the socioeconomic trends we feel will influence the planning of a profitable strategy. Each of these has been discussed and applied to a forecast to be used in evaluating sourcing opportunities in various parts of the world in the coming decade. The chapter is largely based on our own knowledge and view of major trends and, except where noted, we accept the responsibility if our opinions prove to be misleading.

Tom Hickman

CONTENTS

INTRODUCTION

The results of forcing the USSR to choose between guns and butter has clearly succeeded beyond the wildest expectations of the U.S. government. The collapse of communism wasn't the loss of an arms race, but of a spending race. The United States spent more, but very nearly at the expense of its own economy, so that it is entering the 90s as the world's largest debtor nation, having won this economic war without the help of allies.

After World War II the Marshall Plan offered hope to the shattered nations of Europe as hundreds of millions of dollars created markets out of the chaos. In the 1990s, however, the need is for hundreds of *billions*, not just for the USSR, which says it needs a hundred billion to continue restructuring and hold off the forces that threaten a return to dictatorship, but also for Eastern Europe, whose needs are no less. This time, though, the money isn't there.

The USSR may get the hundred billion, but it will come in the form of export loan guarantees or other support that will be tied to increasing democratization. Eastern Europe will receive the same assurances: no money but lots of credit.

All they will need is customers, but they will be facing stiff competition. As for the United States, statistics from its Department of Commerce show that two-thirds of U.S. imports come from 12 nations, half of them in Asia. The others are neighbors, Canada and Mexico, or the major nations of Europe with which the United States shares its culture—England, Germany, France, and Italy. Breaking into the following top-12 club will be difficult.

1. Japan
2. Canada

3. Mexico
4. West Germany
5. Taiwan
6. South Korea
7. United Kingdom
8. France
9. China
10. Italy
11. Hong Kong
12. Singapore

Furthermore, U.S. manufacturers are beginning to successfully woo back customers lost to their foreign competitors. The U.S. dollar is weaker and buys less overseas. In the early 1970s a dollar would buy 360 yen, and the cost of living in Japan was low. Now it's worth 130 yen, and Japan is among the most expensive places in the world. The U.S. manufacturer is also recognizing what it takes to ensure quality. "Good enough" is no longer good enough, and both the buyer and seller know it.

This is the situation of the buyer at the beginning of the 90s. Once synonymous with "cheap and inferior," imported goods now command high prices for their quality. It is no longer possible to buy overseas with a strong dollar, import a cheap product of questionable quality, and use or sell it with impunity. Although there are still many opportunities to buy profitably offshore, it cannot be done as effortlessly as in the past. Purchasing offshore will increasingly require identifying which countries or regions offer the particular advantages needed for a given product or service; rigorously qualifying suppliers for the performance needed to meet today's quality, price, and delivery performance; and closely managing every aspect of the purchase. If they ever were, the "good old days" of easy offshore buying are gone.

CHAPTER 1

BUYING IN THE COMING
GLOBAL ECONOMY

- A buyer from a major New York State tableware company was negotiating for fine crystalware in Czechoslovakia six weeks *before* the fall of the Communist government.
- Ten years after IBM and Coca-Cola withdrew from India because of restrictive trade practices, DEC, Hewlett-Packard, Siemens, and others are investing heavily in manufacturing there.
- A growing photodetector manufacturer in Southern California, dissatisfied with poor quality and delivery from the Philippines, pays more in Singapore but gets better quality and on-time delivery.
- The New Taiwan dollar appreciated almost 50 percent versus the U.S. dollar within a year after martial law was abandoned in Taiwan. Companies locating and buying goods and services there saw their costs rising even more.

How do companies know where the next sourcing opportunities will be? How can they anticipate changes that will increase costs or inhibit production? Where will sourcing-dependent companies look for various types of products and services—low-cost labor, specific technologies, assembly capability? During the coming decade skills in identifying potential producers will be increasingly important in making procurement decisions.

American business has bought offshore for many decades, seeking lower costs, higher productivity, fast product introduction times, and high quality. In the 1990s it will be increasingly difficult to identify overseas sources that will continue to offer real opportunities for these advantages. Many countries are rapidly moving away from cheap labor economies and into high-technology industry to sustain their growth. Industries operating at or near capacity are less flexible and slower to respond than before. The advantages of buying offshore are still available and will continue to be in the future. Finding them in a potential long-term partner will be harder. The following forecast may serve to identify where, and why, to look for some of the procurement opportunities in the next 10 years.

The forecast addresses only the next 5 to 10 years and only those countries or areas with the greatest potential for procurement. It does not address many areas of the world where either political or economic conditions do not appear to offer good sourcing opportunities during the next decade. These include the Middle East, where continuing rivalries will prevent a stable environment, and all of Africa, because of both economic underdevelopment and political instability.

CRITERIA FOR SELECTING SOURCE LOCATIONS

The countries that have the best performance as exporters share these characteristics:

- political stability,
- a well-developed infrastructure, and
- a well-educated, urban work force.

Whereas this combination of attributes does not ensure export success and may be found in many countries not noted for exports, it is the best profile for low-risk procurement success. There is no reason to expect this profile to change and a number of countries will begin to display the profile during the next few years.

Political Stability

Stability, not form of government, is the most important attribute of the political profile. Capitalism has thrived well in Taiwan,

Korea, and elsewhere under dictatorships, and there are probably more socialist democracies than capitalist ones. Thailand is a monarchy. All of these countries have been good trading partners. A number of Latin American countries have offered very poor sources because of their instability, despite ostensibly being both democratic and capitalist.

To the buyer, political stability offers several advantages. Foreign capital, whether private or from international development funds, will contribute to currency and interest rate stability. Together, they mean consistent availability of funds to the vendor and uninterrupted production to the buyer. Work stoppages, particularly in the volatile transportation industries, are generally minimal in stable political climates, ensuring a smooth flow of raw material, transportation of workers, and the shipment of product.

A government's position on trade is important. Those governments which clearly wish to participate in the global economy tend to show greater respect for intellectual property rights, maintain reasonable foreign exchange policies, and have fewer restrictive trade and investment practices. In practice, this is often reflected in the service, or lack of it, provided by the bureaucracies responsible for import or export documentation and other commercial transactions requiring government involvement.

Whether seeking new sources or maintaining existing ones, alert buyers will monitor events in areas of interest. Most national news and business magazines regularly report political and economic conditions in developing countries, especially those where changes indicate new marketing and sourcing opportunities may occur. Many newspapers now include at least a weekly review of global developments with much the same information. Truly global coverage can be found in the *Economist* and the *Herald Tribune*. The Asian *Wall Street Journal* is an excellent publication from which to monitor changes in the Far East.

Infrastructure

A good source location will have a well-developed transportation system and facilities, dependable communications and power distribution, adequate facilities for banking and finance, and consistent service industries supporting all of these.

The reliability of the infrastructure is more important than its complexity or sophistication. In locations offering low-cost labor and little technology, neither can be expected. In many parts of the world it is still necessary to book international telephone calls well in advance and inadequate power exists to support such amenities as air-conditioning. The need to book a call, however, need not seriously affect a transaction. In fact, many people find themselves better prepared for such phone conversations because they must plan for the single opportunity. The lack of reliable services, however, will mean that commitments are not readily made or consistently met. Suppliers within reliable systems, however archaic they may seem, will have learned to use them.

On the other hand, even with the will to become an exporting nation, the lack of facilities to support the process will pose serious problems. The inability to move freight or people efficiently can wreak havoc on a supplier's ability to receive production or packaging materials on time and to maintain regular manufacturing or operations staff.

Poor communications capabilities limit a supplier's ability to perform. An impaired ability to place and expedite orders, arrange and monitor delivery, confirm financing or credit, and make shipments will be reflected in continued and unmanageable delays. Poor international communications will slow the placement of orders, make changes or corrections difficult, and will become particularly exasperating when problems or other urgent reasons to communicate arise.

Adequate banking structures are needed to ensure the flow of money to support a supplier's domestic and international transactions. Where timing or other chronic problems exist in executing checks, drafts, or remittances, local vendors of materials and supplies are likely to hold deliveries or delay production until payment is assured. Opening or confirming letters of credit is often slow where these functions are limited to few, or even to central, banks.

Common statistics, such as the number of telephones, automobiles, or television sets per person, provide a relative measure of the infrastructure of a country. Visitors to a country can develop a fairly accurate assessment through use of its transportation and telephone facilities.

Work Force

A large, well-educated labor pool is as necessary for supplier reliability as either a stable political environment or a supportive infrastructure. Look for an urban concentration of the work force. Lacking an extensive and reliable transportation system, normally an urban phenomenon anyway, supplier capacity will be limited, and, in remote sites, worker attendance will be sporadic and replacement difficult.

Formal education is rarely a requirement for assembly line operations, but the lack of a well-educated work force in a prospective source country will present serious obstacles. In addition to limiting supervisory and managerial skills at the supplier level of the economy, the lack of education will appear as dysfunctions throughout the sourcing process. Orders, invoices, shipments, and banking transactions that are slow and error-prone exacerbate the problems of sourcing offshore. A poorly educated work force may be reflected in rigorous and inflexible procedures that are intended to compensate for the weakness in the system.

Two good measures of the educational level of a country, literacy rate and university student population, reveal that virtually all of the newly industrialized countries have an 80 percent to 90 percent literacy rate and university populations approaching or exceeding 2,000 students per 100,000 inhabitants. Appendix 1 profiles all of the countries included in our forecast plus several others and includes comparative data of each of the major industrial nations as well. It is unlikely the buyer new to doing business offshore would be doing business anywhere else unless the purchase objective was geography-specific raw materials or commodities.

MAJOR TRENDS IN DEVELOPMENT OF THE GLOBAL ECONOMY

Countries offering new source opportunities in the future will probably emerge because of one or both of two major trends: the cascading of industrialization through investment and technology from the developed nations; and increasing attempts to achieve industrial success by emulating Japan.

Cascading Industrialization

Japan's postwar development is probably the most important phenomenon to shape the global economy during the last half century. Its success contributed heavily to the success of Korea, Taiwan, Hong Kong, and Singapore (the "Four Tigers") as well. Japan has provided both money for their development and a model for their economic planning. To plan successfully for the 1990s, however, the sourcing professional needs to recognize that this is a continuing phenomenon. The Four Tigers themselves are now funding development in other parts of Asia. Some understanding of this process is necessary to identify future areas of sourcing opportunity.

With virtually no natural resources, Japan's economic success was built on "value-added" exports. For decades profits were plowed back into the businesses that generated them and into Japan's infrastructure. Very little trickled down to the employees. Promotion and advancement were a uniformly slow progression for everyone. Even the gap between executive and worker was not great except for some lavish expense accounts reserved for the top performers. Corporations still continue to pay paltry dividends.

Whenever possible, production efficiency was increased to offset increasing labor costs, but some work could not readily be automated. In the early 1970s, for both economic and environmental reasons, the Tanaka government forced a substantial amount of manufacturing out of the heavily populated centers of Tokyo, Osaka, and Nagoya to lower-cost rural areas. Eventually, owing both to the increase in the value of the yen and to wage increases, higher costs forced labor-intensive work out of Japan entirely.

Work and technology continue to flow from the United States and Japan through the same path. The Taiwanese are investing in Thailand and Malaysia to produce electronic cable assemblies, a commodity the Taiwanese have long monopolized, as their domestic labor costs have risen too high to compete effectively. At the same time the Taiwanese are building higher-technology industries in their own country; integrated circuit foundries have started in Taiwan to compete with the Japanese.

Singapore recently started refusing entry to businesses with no research and development (R&D) and it has become a national policy for Singapore to concentrate on intellectual and technological value added. Meanwhile, Singapore's labor-intensive work has been moving across the straits to Malaysia. More significantly, Singapore and others are investing there as well; Singapore is now Malaysia's third biggest foreign investor, after Taiwan and Japan (*Singapore Business Times*, October 5, 1990). Single-sided printed circuit boards, the simple brown ones found in inexpensive radios, can no longer be found in Taiwan and infrequently in Korea, Hong Kong, or Singapore. These localities have shifted their emphasis to double- or multilayer boards. To source single-layer boards a buyer must go elsewhere, such as to Shanghai, which built tremendous capacity for China's television industry and now supplies much of the world's single-sided boards.

This pattern of development not only will continue in the Far East during the 1990s but also will characterize part of the continuing development in Europe and Latin America. Although no single focus country will emerge in Europe, as Japan has done in the Far East, labor-intensive work and successively advanced technology will flow from the advanced nations of Western Europe to both the less-developed Western European nations and those of Eastern Europe. Many Latin American countries are already looking as much to Japan and the Four Tigers as to the United States for a guide to their development programs.

Several factors will accelerate this process. First, a number of changes to encourage foreign investment will occur in the nations most eager for growth. These may include establishing currency convertibility, eliminating or relaxing foreign investment restrictions, and encouraging and facilitating licensing agreements. Those which implement these changes earliest, and also provide a degree of investor security by both recognizing intellectual property rights and providing for reasonable repatriation of profits, will be at the front of the foreign investment curve. Relaxation of restrictions on technology to Eastern Europe by the United States and COCOM* will both support the transfer of technology while virtually ensuring that it will be a cascading process.

JAPAN AS AN ECONOMIC MODEL

The second significant factor in global economic development that will impact source selection in the 1990s will be the conscious selection of Japan as the economic model for growth. In Asia, of course, Japan became the model for the other Asian nations because of its proximity, its investment in the region, and its own success. Elsewhere, the U.S. image is tarnished by its massive deficit; the miserable state of the national health system; the growing and widely publicized problems of homelessness, drugs, and violence; and the increasing disparity between the wealthy and the poor. Conversely, Japan is perceived as an admirable model for growth.

The image Japan has created is virtually the antithesis of that of the United States. Unemployment appears very low, not only because full employment receives support, but also because many of the seasonal employees included in statistics elsewhere are ignored. The yen continues to rise, despite occasional setbacks, because of continual investment in processes, plant, and equipment, and the resultant maintenance or improvement in productivity. Real incomes continue to grow, and Japanese spending worldwide continually advertises its growth. Any problems with drugs, poverty, or discrimination receive little publicity. Supporting this contrast are indications that the United States itself recognizes value in many Japanese approaches to

---

* "The United States participates in an international security export control system. The Coordinating Committee (COCOM) of this system reviews proposed transactions to export or reexport certain strategic commodities or technical data to the People's Republic of China and Country Groups Q, W, and Y." (Sec. 370.11, (2,(c)) U.S. Export Administration Regulations) COCOM participating countries include Belgium, Canada, Denmark, France, the Federal Republic of Germany, Greece, Italy, Japan, Luxembourg, the Netherlands, Norway, Portugal, Turkey and the United Kingdom. Country Groups Q, W, and Y included the U.S.S.R., other Warsaw Pact Countries, Albania, Mongolia, and Laos in the 1990 edition of the regulations.

business. Numerous books and articles propound various Japanese methods of production or management, U.S. business schools offer Japanese business studies, and businesses everywhere study and try to emulate Japanese successes. Japan is already the de facto model for many emerging nations.

The Japanese Model

The economic model appears almost ideal for sustained growth and the accumulation of wealth. Drawn with a broad brush, it consists of five basic elements that combine both national attributes and government form and policy:

These characteristics . . .	*provide these benefits:*
1. Centrally directed economy, a well-defined and nationally accepted mission,	Efficient utilization of national strengths.
2. focused on value-added exports,	Growth opportunity in a nation lacking in natural resources.
3. with a long-term view of growth and profits,	Highly debt leveraged with bank cooperation and involvement. High investment in plant, R&D.
4. implemented by a bureaucracy almost immune to political policy shifts,	Stable environment for business, consistent policy implementation at all levels.
5. supported by a homogenous, well-educated, group-oriented, and highly motivated work force.	Common focus on goals, high productivity, high savings rate and resultant low cost of capital.

Without all the elements that led to Japan's success—its homogeneity, its intense focus on group rather than individual identity, and its work ethic—duplicates of the model will not emerge in countries that copy it. Instead, a subset of the model will appear, particularly where entrenched governments or a variety of ethnic or religious groups preclude total adoption. Certainly, the features that enabled Japan to lead the industrialization of Asia will be expressed as policy: central direction of growth, emphasis on exports and domestic value added, and attention to the benefits of long-term, stable production. It is equally likely that many of the restrictive trade practices will also emerge as policy. At the national level they may also include government subsidies to export industries and attempts to protect domestic markets, manage exchange rates, impose onerous conditions on licensing, or limit currency convertibility.

To the buyer this may create both opportunities and obstacles. Strong export emphasis may be supported by export or industry subsidies, reducing the buyer's cost. Misapplied, such emphasis may mean weak protection of intellectual property rights, requiring extra caution on the part of purchasers to protect proprietary designs. Policies designed to protect foreign reserves by managing trade balances may result in difficult inward customs clearance, even of material intended for re-export.

At the individual supplier level, too, many negotiating tactics of the Japanese will be affected. The practice of requesting target pricing is already becoming widespread. Quotations are initiated with severe payment and delivery terms and long lead times, forcing buyers to negotiate uphill even to terms and conditions normal in the United States. Long-term, high-volume orders will be sought and discouraging prices quoted for anything less. The most successful suppliers will begin to establish a presence in the United States to capture not only manufacturing profits but those of managing the shipment, distribution, and some of the marketing efforts as well. Some familiarity with Japanese practices will be increasingly helpful in doing business anywhere in the world.

FORECAST

Eastern Europe

Eastern European nations will be particularly prone to adopt elements of the Japanese model, if only because they are actively seeking new economic and political models. There are a number of reasons to believe the model could be adopted almost intact and for redevelopment of the region to follow the pattern of the Far East.

Recent descriptions of the economic state of much of Eastern Europe have compared it to the war-torn economies of the Allies immediately after the Second World War. There have even been frequent references to the need for a new Marshall Plan to help speed the recovery of the region. Despite the political hype that may accompany the occasional billions that will be dumped into the area, the effort won't approach the scope of the original Marshall Plan. More likely, in proportion to the global economy now and then, the billions will be little more than pump priming. The economic development of Eastern Europe will more closely resemble that of the Far East.

Japan, after the War, didn't enjoy the social status of the Americans' European second cousins and was not seen as a large future market, two of the imperatives of the Marshall Plan. Its postwar development received a lot of direction from the Occupation but little external funding. Redevelopment was carefully nurtured bit by bit. Whole industries were rebuilt at the piece-part level; perhaps a hundred households made one of the hundreds of tiny parts for sewing machines to be assembled in a small workshop. On the relative scale of the original Marshall Plan, the redevelopment of Eastern Europe will be closer to that of Japan.

Several other parallels can be drawn between Japan and Eastern Europe. The fall of the Communists may have the same impact as the breakup of the Zaibatsu, the huge industrial companies that dominated the Japanese economy before the War. Removing the entire executive and most of the managerial tiers of a nation's economy without a replacement, whatever economic system may be in place at the time, requires years to overcome. This was the case in Japan and may be the case in Eastern Europe if, in their lust for ideological purity, overzealous reformers throw out all their managers in the bath.

Like Japan, Eastern Europe will also be moving toward democracy with a population that has never had a voice. The control the military had over prewar Japan and the communist control of Eastern Europe were very similar. Eastern Europe will also be undertaking land reform and economic reforms unprecedented except in postwar Japan.

A few strong contrasts can be drawn as well. MacArthur had, literally, an army of professionals to support his reforms. Hundreds of experts on government, economics, the judiciary, and, of course, business are already peddling their skills in Eastern Europe. Their efforts can only be fragmented and uncoordinated, and they certainly won't resemble the cohesive effort of the Occupation. Moreover, given the mix of governments and private consultants vying for influence or profit in Europe, many of the projects will be conflicting, mired in bureaucracy, or simply ineffective.

Despite the massive failure of state planning in the USSR, the Eastern European states will probably rely heavily on state guidance during reconstruction because of its success in Japan. A recent First Secretary in the U.S. Embassy in Tokyo frequently referred to Japan as the "World's Second Largest Centrally Directed Economy." If the Ministry of International Trade and Industry's (MITI) "guidance" isn't state planning, it is as close as will be found outside communist countries and will lend credibility to the approach, especially to countries unfamiliar with any other system. Doing business of any sort, including sourcing, will include tedious interaction with government agencies.

The several generations who have lived under the socialist economics of communist rule will be reluctant to abandon quickly the lifelong security the system offered. Rather than opting for the potentially massive individual rewards that unfettered capitalism might offer, the emerging democracies will probably perpetuate social security. In the context of developing opportunities for sourcing in Eastern Europe, such programs will mean higher costs from a variety of taxes. Individuals will be taxed at a greater rate, adding to labor costs, and products will be taxed, probably in the form of value-added taxes (VAT) already common in Western Europe. Although the basic wages of Eastern Europe will mean initially low labor costs, the costs of rebuilding these ravaged economies while maintaining a large degree of individual security point to rapidly rising costs later in the decade.

The redevelopment of East Germany's economy will be unique because of reunification. Some of the impacts, and problems, of this process are already becoming evident. West Germany is already providing massive funding to help support the rapidly deteriorating economy of East Germany. Although the government announced that benefits would cease in the summer of 1990, unemployment benefits were paid to immigrants of East Germany, many of whom did not have the skills, experience, or motivation to seek the few available jobs. Taxes will increase for those that can pay them (i.e., the West Germans) to pay for these subsidies and others. Heavy investment will be needed to restore the East German infrastructure, for health care, for example, pollution control, and for numerous other problems. Wages will be under pressure in West Germany as immigration from the East pushes up unemployment or jobs move into the lower-wage areas of East Germany. Interest rates will probably rise through central bank controls to curb inflation.

These pressures may manifest themselves in sporadic displays of social unrest. Nevertheless, Germany is probably better poised to implement its own restoration than any of its neighbors. Although the economic pressures will be intense, both populations have waited too long for reunification to let it fail. Exports and investment will be encouraged to secure the capital needed to fund redevelopment. The pressure on wages and the availability of a large, well-educated, and highly motivated work force will ensure success. The offshore buyer will be able to source a wide variety of quality, high-technology products.

Three major factors will dominate the development of the other Eastern European nations during the 1990s: (1) their prewar economic and political relationships; (2) their current economic condition; and (3) the political and economic naiveté of both their governments and people. All three will tend to slow any expansion of the European Economic Community (EEC) to include the Eastern Europeans.

Some degree of suspicion toward Germany will lead Poland and Czechoslovakia to approach any involvement with the EEC slowly, especially since German reunification will probably lead it to a dominant role in the EEC. Since the EEC is so highly politicized, most of the Eastern European countries will, initially, be rather diffident in approaching relations with it.

The tremendous need for capital will be the strongest factor slowing relationships with the EEC. Most of the Eastern European countries will want to avoid a close relationship with the EEC to ensure that the United States and Japan, the largest potential investor nations, perceive that they will receive equal status with the other nations of Europe. At most, they will probably seek the sort of association Turkey enjoys with the Community.

Czechoslovakia, the third largest industrial nation in Europe before the war and the one with the highest standard of living in the Eastern bloc, will progress most rapidly. For the offshore buyer, this will not only mean that sources can be developed there more quickly, but that costs will increase more rapidly as well. Poland and Hungary will follow, at first with products such as are now available from the Newly Industrialized Countries (NICs) of the Far East. The progress of growth will mimic that of the Far East, with the lesser-developed countries following in the footsteps of the more advanced ones. Development in Bulgaria and Romania will be delayed by the ethnic rivalry that has long characterized the area.

The Soviet Union

The development of the USSR as a potential source will proceed along a far different path than that of Eastern Europe. Gorbachev's *perestroika* and *glasnost* provided the window of opportunity for change in both Eastern Europe and the Soviet Union, but the reasons differ markedly. The Eastern European countries have been Soviet-dominated states yearning for freedom. Although their economies have clearly been devastated by 40 years of misrule, most had burgeoning industrial economies before the war, their economic development had generally paralleled that of Western Europe, and they had been developing skilled industrial workers and management. Eastern Europe's role within the Soviet bloc has largely been the transformation of Russian and other Soviet Republics' raw material into finished products.

The nation on which Lenin forced communism had been

largely agrarian. Those who saw the movie *Dr. Zhivago* may remember the close resemblance between the situation and life-style depicted and historical portrayals of the United States before and during the Civil War. The impression was largely accurate. Certainly, the distinction is not black and white. Never-theless, Russia, the easternmost nation in Europe, greatly lagged behind the rest of Europe in industrializing. The massive spend-ing of the Soviet Union in its defense industries has done little to prepare Russia to compete equally with the rest of the in-dustrialized world. Internally, Gorbachev has responded to the virtual absence of consumer goods in an agrarian economy hardly able to feed the country, much less export, and an in-frastructure that can't support distribution for either.

The Soviet economy will change. Whether Gorbachev or Yeltsin will accomplish restructuring the economy or change is forced on some successor is almost immaterial unless, of course, the change is violent. Even so, glasnost, perestroika, and the events and successes of Eastern Europe ensure some measure of market freedom. Moreover, whatever its impact on the Soviet Union, the Three Day Putsch will have little effect on sourcing from the region. The Southern tier of Republics may become the Northern tier of Islam; the problems of buying from either will have changed only in the form the bureaucracy takes. Major opportunities will be found in the Republics that remain in the Union, whatever form it may take, and stay within the purview of historical Russia.

Foreign ownership will probably not play much of a role in the development of this economy. Russian nationalism will dom-inate Russian politics. Because of the lack of natural barriers, a history of invasion, from Genghis Kahn to Nazi Germany, has bred a suspicion of foreigners little understood outside Russia. It was probably Gorbachev the Russian as much as Gorbachev the Communist speaking when he pointed out to President Bush that he had not asked for help. The process will therefore be much slower than the economic development of Eastern Europe.

Sourcing opportunities in Russia will therefore be found in situations that support the growth of industry, not merely the purchase of labor. Purchases that involve capital formation will be welcome. Supplying technology, tools, or know-how will generally be a key to developing a source. Genady Gerasimov on "Face the Nation" clearly stated that the Soviet Union wants investment, technology, and help in developing management skills, not aid. Even if aid is needed to help the country through some miserable winters, sourcing strategies should focus on providing technology and skills.

It may even be possible to develop a long-term partnership based on near-obsolete technology. Many companies have moved obsolete tools into lesser-developed countries, especially as automated assembly techniques were developed to offset rising labor costs. The Volkswagen Beetle, which continued in South America long after its disappearance in the United States, is probably the best-known example. Rather than having to re-tool an entire factory for automation and retrain its workers for a new technology, laying off many of them as a result, near-obsolete tooling may be a welcome path to development.

Moves toward a free market economy in the Soviet Union, even one that is allowed to develop more slowly, also could allow the Soviet Union to take advantage of its geographic proximity to both Eastern Europe and the Far East as a source of raw materials and commodity foods. Although somewhat colder than the Great Plains of the United States, the steppes of Russia could readily supplant them as a source of winter wheat if farmed the same way. The tiaga, a forested tier stretching across Russia between the steppes and the tundra, offers immense timber reserves for both markets as well. By the end of the 1990s, the United States may encounter considerable competition in the timber and grain markets of the Far East and Europe. Nikolai Petrakov, Gorbachev's economic adviser, has said that "with our forestry resources, if we had modern technology we could flood the world with cheap paper" (interview in *Forbes* Magazine, 7 May 1990, p. 117).

The Far East

The relative positions of the player nations in the Far East will remain constant through the 1990s, although the technological level of each will continue to grow.

Japan will remain at the forefront in exports and technology.

Technology-added will begin to supplant *value-added* as the main component in export value as Japan's research investments and patents grow into mature products. Whether directly, in the form of licenses, or as a component cost for products available only from Japan, technology will represent a significant part of Japan's exports. Japan will be the only source for some products at the leading edge in electronics, optics, machine tools, and ceramics and will continue to dominate the markets of high-volume, process-intensive commodities such as computer memories. Japan's products will be available almost exclusively through subsidiary companies outside Japan or through the many large trading companies.

Korea, Taiwan, Hong Kong, and Singapore will displace Japan in many markets it now dominates. They will master the current technologies and produce at lower cost than Japan's rising wages will permit; Taiwan and Korea because they still lag far behind Japan in income, Hong Kong by producing in China. Singapore, in particular, will also focus increasingly on technology. It is already offering itself as an alternative to Hong Kong to well-educated Chinese reluctant to risk contact with China.

All of these will also continue to cascade their work and technology into other countries of Asia. Malaysia, Indonesia, Thailand, and the Philippines have been providing low-cost manufacturing labor, often building products from kits of material shipped in from another country, for many years. More recently, substantial investment has been made to produce a wide range of products as their manufacturing cost rose in the more highly industrialized countries. These include electronic components, wire and cable, and molded plastics as well as more complex assemblies.

All of these countries share much of the profile of a good source location. They have literacy rates near or above 90 percent. Except for the Philippines, all have concentrated urban populations. All have large university populations and are expected to continue strong emphasis on education.

From a sourcing viewpoint, perceived political stability is about the only factor that distinguishes these nations from one other. Despite the apparent fragility of government in the Philippines since Marcos, there has been a stable government there for many years, albeit one nobody seemed to be pleased with. Nevertheless, business flourished and few people want to reverse this process. The problems in the Philippines stem largely from the lack of infrastructure development; too much of the nation's wealth was siphoned off into corruption and graft. The greatest threats have come from the conservative elements, those who feel the government is not moving fast enough to correct the restraints on growth.

Much the same situation should occur in Indonesia where, under Sukarno and Suharto, almost four decades of stability have been enforced in much the same way Marcos did it in the Philippines. The more recent economic improvements in Indonesia, however, have been made with Suharto's support and actually represent a change in direction from the graft, corruption, and closed borders associated with the country. Expect continued progress in business and economic conditions, especially if there is an orderly change in government after Suharto. Even if there is not, a strong likelihood exists that, as in the Philippines, any new government will recognize the need for continuity in the business and industrial sectors of the economy.

The Association of South Eastern Asian Nations (ASEAN) will continue to grow in strength and importance. Singapore, Malaysia and Indonesia have already begun a trilateral association which includes Singapore; Johor, the Malaysian Sultanate just across the causeway from Singapore; and Batam, an Indonesian island easily accessible from Singapore by ferry. All of ASEAN plans to form an economic community similar to the EEC within the next fifteen years.

Throughout the Far East, many of the factors that characterized Japan's industrial development will be present as well, notably (1) strong efforts to improve national infrastructure, (2) increasing emphasis on intellectual and technological strength, and (3) occasional nontariff barriers to protect and perpetuate growth. There will be some attempts to limit wage growth, but few will be successful because the national traits that supported this phenomenon in Japan are rarely found elsewhere. Job-hopping for increased pay has become so common in Singapore that businesspeople are only half-joking when they ask, "How many of your workers came back from lunch today?" The funding for development must therefore come through taxation. Combined wage growth, increased taxes, and the currency appreciation that accompanies success will lead to continual price increases during the 1990s.

A search for further sourcing opportunities elsewhere in Asia should consider the common denominators of the countries just discussed: (1) a low-cost, concentrated labor pool; (2) a growing emphasis on education, infrastructure development, and other adjuncts to industrialization; and (3) the political stability needed to focus on long-term goals. In addition, they will all have the most important ingredient common to all the nations that have succeeded: aggressive businesspeople hungry for success.

A few other countries in the region offer most of these qualities. India has been a fairly stable democracy for many years, has a growing student population, and is recovering some of the many young Indians educated abroad, eager to capitalize on India's prospects. There is a huge, very low-wage labor pool, and the Indian government will lend up to 85 percent to Indians willing to employ workers in export-directed ventures.

Sri Lanka had sustained an economic program similar to those of other developing countries in Asia for some years before it was interrupted by the Tamil insurgency. Given a return to stability, sourcing prospects for labor-intensive products will be good there. Pakistan, assuming some relief from the pressures of supporting neighboring Afghanistan, may be in a position similar to that of India.

Products that could be reliably sourced in this last group of countries will probably fall into two narrow categories: (1) simple assemblies or fabrications having a high, repetitive labor content and minimal plant, tool, or manufacturing fixtures or (2) products from a manufacturer who has made significant plant investment and will subcontract assembly. Procurement will be a lengthy process, involving detailed instructions and training, extensive communications, and many unforeseen obstacles. Expect lengthy delays, poor initial quality, and irregular performance. Not surprisingly, these problems were exactly what early investors in the Four Tigers experienced and are just now being overcome in Thailand and Malaysia. To reap the same rewards, a prospective buyer must be prepared to encounter the same problems.

China

With the tremendous attention that has been given to the People's Republic of China since President Nixon reestablished diplomatic relations, and the incident at Tiananmen Square, China deserves separate attention in the review of sourcing opportunities in the Far East.

China compares very poorly with the other nations of Asia under all of the criteria identified for potential success. Its infrastructure is in miserable condition. Few roads are paved, there are few trucks to use them, and "central planning" uses the trucks inefficiently. Rail traffic is limited to routes between major cities, largely the legacy of the European railroads of the last century. Air traffic is poorly coordinated; tickets often must be purchased at each stage of a domestic journey and reservations are unreliable. Communication is difficult; telephone and telex facilities are frequently available only in community centers, not at places of business. At present, the country lacks enough capacity to make enough copper wire for its own power and communications requirements this century. From a sourcing standpoint, the difficulty of communicating orders, specifications, and changes and of moving people or material makes most other alternatives preferable to China.

China's literacy rate is low and several factors will tend to retard its improvement. Since the Communists came to power in 1949 suspicion of intellectuals has been intense; this was a peasant revolution. The Cultural Revolution reflected some of this attitude. Moreover, the government appears to foment this attitude to help perpetuate its power. Tiananmen Square was probably no exception; the students started the movement, workers followed. Last, the mere task of training enough teachers, especially to work in rural areas, will take far more than the years remaining in this decade. The difficulty of finding, training, and keeping skilled workers will make sourcing very difficult.

The political climate does not enhance the prospects for business. Heading a business-related organization is less desirable than holding a political position near power. Corruption in politics is rampant and, therefore, so is the financial reward of being in politics. Among the few prerequisites of managing a business is the potential for graft. Since the Tiananmen Square incident, the possibility of raising even unwarranted suspicion is impeding any communication with foreigners, because any suspicion might impede possible political advancement.

The "Iron Rice Bowl" has been a disincentive to performance and adds greatly to cost. Bonuses are invariably paid; the targets for most enterprises are set so low that they are always paid. To keep everyone employed, three to five times as many employees are assigned to a position as are actually needed for the task, effectively multiplying by three to five the cost to perform it.

Nevertheless, the patient buyer will find sourcing opportunities in China. Taiwanese firms are already complaining about their inability to compete with the mainland's low labor costs; the mainland has now replaced Taiwan as the United States' largest shoe supplier because its wages are only about a fourth of Taiwan's (*China Post*, 21 January 1991). Buyers who will have successful relationships in the next decade will have begun those relationships in the 1990s, both discovering the problems described above and learning how to deal with them. Firms who plan to start marketing there in the 1990s, hoping to reap the benefits of a tremendous market in the future, should plan to source there as well. Given China's meager foreign reserves, some quid pro quo will be expected of those hoping to sell to China.

The areas of opportunity are already becoming evident. Guangdong province, sometimes facetiously called Northern Hong Kong, does virtually all of the electronics subcontracting for Hong Kong firms. Shanghai is currently the world's largest producer of single-sided printed circuit boards and has reasonably efficient capacity for double- and some multilayer boards as well. Beijing is constructing extensive industrial parks near the city with plans to ensure both equipment and a trained work force. Moreover, it is focusing on developing high-tech, export-oriented firms and, despite what is happening in the footwear and similar industries, does not welcome investment in what it calls "sunset industries" (*Singapore Straits Times*, 10 October 1990).

In all of these cases, little local material, technology, or skill can be assumed. The buyer must plan to provide kits for assembly if anything more than the simplest components or commodity materials are required. A need for exhaustive training should be anticipated, not only for the production staff but for supervisory, technical, and quality positions as well.

Buyers in China should recognize that the country is still intensely regional and that ventures that rely on participation from many different locations could be severely disrupted during a period of unrest. Guangdong, Shanghai, and Beijing, for example, all promote themselves independently, much as different cities in the U.S. do. Instability at the national level of China, however, would very likely disrupt communications, transportation and financial transactions between its regions and cities. A failure at the national level could be even more severe and see the nation deteriorate into the sort of factional feuding that has generally characterized dynastic changes in China. Given the failure of Communism in Eastern Europe and the Soviet Union, and the disintegration that followed it, such a change in China is not unthinkable.

Australia and New Zealand

The other two countries in this region of the world that meet all of the requirements for success are Australia and New Zealand. They haven't been addressed so far only because they don't fit in the pattern of development outlined for the rest of Asia.

Australia and New Zealand are both in the anomalous position of finding themselves associated with the Western nations because of their English-speaking heritage but competing with the nations of the Far East because of their geography. The cultural relationship of Australia and New Zealand with other English-speaking countries has long dominated their business relationships. Nevertheless, both find themselves in the position of commodity sources for the Far East, exporting ore, timber, wool, and foodstuffs.

A history of strong unions and Labor governments has led both countries to the highest labor rates and lowest productivity in Asia. Recognizing their deteriorating competitive positions and dependence on agriculture and raw materials exports, both Australia and New Zealand have begun extensive economic reforms. During the 1980s, taxes were cut, and price, wage, and currency controls were relaxed.

The offshore buyer will find both countries easy places to do business because neither language nor culture present any obstacles. Unemployment is high, especially in New Zealand, so wages will probably remain stable, especially when compared to the rest of Asia. High wage costs may be offset by lower material costs and the benefits of a well-developed infrastructure. Few attempts will be made to emulate the Japanese. A fierce independence, strong unions, and a strong labor influence on government even when Labor is not in power do not offer a fertile environment for such a transplant.

Latin America

Latin America should offer rich opportunities for American sourcing operations during the 1990s. One simple reason is that it is easier to do business there than in Europe or Asia, where proximity favors the local buyers. The mere fact that the United States is eight or nine time zones away slows communications with both Europe and Asia but is not a factor in sourcing in Latin America.

At the same time, the following factors will combine to create a more favorable environment for procurement in Latin America:

1. Pressures to solve the massive debt problems of the Latin countries will result in structural changes in many of the debtor nations. Some of these will facilitate sourcing.

2. The Western Hemisphere will address the growing regional economic spheres in Europe and the Far East with cooperative measures intended to maintain balance. Many of these will foster sourcing activity in Latin America.

The impetus to accelerate economic cooperation in the hemisphere is twofold: the miserable state of most Latin American economies and the need to counteract the competitive effects of the EEC's open trade. Among these effects is the fact that Mexico, Brazil, Argentina, and Venezuela are over $300 billion in debt.

The Brady debt-reduction strategy has had the effect of doing little but subsidize our banks' existing loans at U.S. taxpayer expense. Many banks are refusing to make loans, significantly reducing these countries' access to credit. Moreover, many potential lenders see greater opportunity in the developments in Eastern Europe (Peter Truell in *The Wall Street Journal*, 22 January 1990). Double- and triple-digit inflation is common in Latin America. Consumers spend their money as fast as they receive it, before inflation reduces its value. As a result there is little saving and little hope of internal financing.

The countries' individual attempts to correct their problems have been ineffectual. Regular, often violent, changes in government occur under slogans for reform, but few structural improvements result. Latin America continues to have a tremendous gulf between its poor and its wealthy. Many currencies are not convertible, and foreign exchange is often severely restricted. Much of the massive debt service is met by selling natural resources: Mexico's oil, Brazil's forests.

Little of the Japanese model could be made applicable to the situation in most Latin American states. Much of the work force is neither well educated nor urban. Central planning is too often focused on maintaining entrenched power, not solving problems; and the supporting bureaucrats are more often in patronage than career positions. The debt crises of most of the countries overshadow any long-term view of the problems. The few trappings of the model that do exist are generally protectionist and do more to inhibit trade than promote it.

Development in the Far East and Europe will provide a strong impetus for a coordinated approach to Latin America's problems. It will become increasingly apparent during the 1990s that the new, loosely knit economic spheres in Europe and the Far East will have significantly altered the patterns of world trade. Both of these economic communities will include rich, highly industrialized nations and nations with cheap labor, desire for growth, and close access to stable supplies for raw materials. In addition, because of the massive pent-up demand of Eastern Europe and the increasing affluence of the Asian nations, both regions will generate tremendous internal consumer demand during the decade.

Sourcing in both areas will more and more frequently reflect competition for production capacity as the United States loses its preeminence as the world's consumer. Fewer products will be tailored exclusively for the U.S. market, and many will bear the extra cost of features or requirements needed to market in Europe or the Far East. Among the added costs, for example, will be those of obtaining and maintaining regulatory agency approvals. In addition to Underwriters' Laboratories (UL) or Federal Communications Commission (FCC) approvals, more suppliers will also seek VDE or TUV (Germany) and JIS or VCCI (Japan) agency approvals to facilitate selling outside the United States.

The 1990s will see an American policy initiative recognizing the increasing power of regional economic cooperation in the Far East and Europe and seeking to meet that increasing power of cooperation with increased economic cooperation in the Western Hemisphere. Policy will concurrently address the growing economic crisis in the Central and South American countries. Because no U.S. administration will wish to appear as abandoning America's global posture to one of regional defense, the emphasis of the policy will be on cooperation rather than community. This emphasis will also be needed to secure cooperation; Latin America resents any domination or interference by the United States.

The policy will essentially exchange favorable access to U.S. markets for economic changes exacted from any country wishing to participate. American business has long been frustrated by inadequate protection of intellectual property rights, restrictive foreign exchange policies, and the difficulty of repatriating profits. From a national viewpoint, policies that support and enhance the development of a middle class will be seen as necessary for economic growth. Some sort of debt relief would add an extra incentive to participate while trade credits, development loans, and other devices would encourage growth.

The likely participants in such a process are those countries that are both carrying large debt or have already developed significant industry: Brazil, Venezuela, and, possibly, Argentina, Chile, and Costa Rica. A broader view of Latin American development would recognize these countries as foci to cascade development to other nations. The Bush Administration's "Enterprise for the Americas" includes a series of bilateral "framework agreements" signed with individual countries in the region (*Business Week*, 24 December 1990). This structure clearly indicates that, although the initiative is ostensibly hemispheric, the United States will reward nations individually for progress toward U.S. goals.

The United States and Canada have essentially opened their borders to trade, preempting even the EEC in reducing internal tariffs; the few controls that remain address only sensitive weapons technology. In June 1990 Presidents Bush and Salinas announced the beginning of talks to seek a free trade pact between the United States and Mexico (*Wall Street Journal*, 6 June 1990). The subsequent discussions appear to focus largely on Mexico as the United States' southern neighbor rather than on regional trade. In February 1991, Canada agreed to join the United States in its free trade negotiations with Mexico, ensuring at least a North American counterbalance to the EEC. Both the agreement with Canada and the one under negotiation with Mexico have much the same effect as the EEC agreements. Both the EEC agreement and the U.S./Canadian treaty reduce regional tariffs and protect regional trade, but neither can readily be described as raising protectionist barriers. As labor costs continue to rise in the Far East and the Eastern European countries develop, an early start sourcing in Latin America may prove to be a wise decision, especially if tariffs are reduced in the Western Hemisphere.

SUMMARY

Countries that have the best potential to offer stable and reliable sources of supply generally share three characteristics: a high degree of political stability; a well-developed infrastructure; and a well-educated, urban work force.

The progress of economic development follows a pattern of cascading industrialization as developed nations continually seek lower labor-cost markets. The pattern is clearly evident in Asia, where the United States and Japan first moved production to

Taiwan, Hong Kong, Korea, and Singapore. Each of these countries have since begun to farm out their own labor-intensive industry, to Thailand, Malaysia, and Indonesia, for example. Cascading technology will follow in the same course.

Because of its success, and the apparent absence of the crime and drug problems of the United States, Japan will be the dominant model for developing nations. Few countries will succeed entirely in emulating Japan because of its unique cultural heritage, but many will try some central economic direction and will attempt various means to protect their domestic industries.

Cascading industrialization and elements of the Japanese model will characterize development in Eastern Europe. A new Marshall Plan is unlikely because of the enormity of the problem and the weak economies of the West. The pattern will more likely be private Western investment and domestic grass roots industry.

The decade will see increasing polarization of super-regional trade agreements. Free trade within the European Economic Community serves to inhibit imports from anywhere else without being blatantly protectionist. In response, the United States and Canada have already reached a free trade agreement and the United States and Mexico are actively pursuing one. Latin America will be encouraged to participate. The developed nations of Asia, already somewhat protectionist, will avoid overt measures to inhibit imports but will probably begin to react to the EEC and Western Hemisphere communities in the 90s.

CHECKLIST

Political Stability
> Consistent government policies toward business.
> Peaceful changes of government.

Infrastructure
> Easy telephone or fax and mail communications.
> Adequate highways, rail, and port facilities.
> Adequate reliable worker transportation.

Work Force
> Large, well-educated labor pool.

Urban concentration; no abnormal commute, shopping time.

An abnormal amount of worker training will not be required.

Level of Industrialization

Consistent with the proposed purchase.

Is the country or region exporting raw materials or has it exported value-added products?

Level of Technology

Consistent with the proposed purchase?

Will suppliers attempt high-technology production on preindustrial equipment?

Government influence

Are exchange controls rigid?

Government influence on pricing?

Ministry review of contracts?

External Alternatives

Is another, or are other countries' purchasing profiles better suited to the proposed purchase?

Are anticipated trade agreements likely to have a favorable or adverse influence on proposed purchases in the future?

APPENDIX 1A: PROFILES OF LIKELY SUPPLIER COUNTRIES

The following is an example of the data available for sourcing decisions. **Source of Data:** Georg P. Muller, *Comparative World Data: A Statistical Handbook for Social Science*, Baltimore & London: Johns Hopkins University Press. (also available on diskette) NOTE: All data is as of 1980; socialist countries generally do not report Gross Domestic Product data.

The collection of data covering nearly every country in the world is sorted by 51 variables.

Examples of specific variables include: per capita income; telephones per thousand population; adult literacy; duration of schooling; population; gross domestic product (GDP); foreign property as a percentage of GDP; share of exports supplied by manufacturers; lack of civil liberties; amount of political rights; protest demonstrations; agriculture's share of GDP; industrial production's share of GDP; services' share of GDP.

For each variable, a clear and concise definition is given and the source of information for each is noted.

V1: Income per capita, expressed in U.S.$ per capita, using 1980 exchange rates and constant prices. Population in million capita.

V2: Number of telephones per thousand inhabitants.

V5: Adult literacy, expressed as the percentage share of the population aged 15 and over that is able to both read and write.

V6: Duration of schooling, expressed as the average time spent on the acquisition of primary and secondary education.

V16: Population, expressed as the number of people de facto living in the country.

V17: Gross domestic product: expressed in U.S.$ and valued at constant prices and at 1980 exchange rates.

V25: Foreign property as a percentage of GDP, as a measure of stocks of foreign direct investment by Development Assistance Committee countries in the given country as a percentage of GDP.

V29: Manufacturing's share of the given country's exports, expressed as the percentage share of the exports of manufacturers in the FOB-value of all exports of the country.

V30: Lack of civil liberties, expressed in a scale from 1 (highest degree of liberty) to 7 (lowest degree of liberty).

V31: Lack of political rights, expressed in a scale from 1 (most political rights) to 7 (least political rights).

V34: Political strikes, expressed as a percentile with 1 (lowest) to 100 (highest). This is interpreted as a further indication of political rights with more strikes (higher percentile) indicating greater freedom of political expression. A political strike is defined as a strike of workers or students against a government and excludes all forms of strikes that aim primarily at a realization of economic goals.

V42: Agriculture's share of GDP, expressed as a percentage of total GDP.

V43: Industry's share of GDP, expressed as a percentage of total GDP.

V44: Services' share of GDP, expressed as a percentage of total GDP.

TABLE 1A
Asia (except Japan in Table 1D)

Variable	Australia	People's Republic of China	India	Indonesia	Korea	Malaysia	New Zealand	Pakistan	Philippines	Singapore	Sri Lanka	Taiwan	Thailand
V1: Income	3617	–	229	460	1646	1662	7471	293	719	4629	267	–	692
V2: Telephone	489	4	4	3	77	45	560	4	15	291	6	–	11
V5: Literacy	–	65.5	34.1	67.3	87.6	–	–	26.2	82.6	82.9	86.1	–	88.0
V6: School	10.8	7.8	6.1	8.6	11.0	9.2	12.2	3.2	9.4	9.7	9.5	–	7.9
V16: Population	14.7	1003	664	151	38.1	13.9	3.1	82.1	48.1	2.4	14.7	–	46.5
V17: GDP	141	–	152	69.5	62.8	23.1	23.2	24.1	34.6	11.2	3.9	–	32.1
V25: Foreign Property	–	–	2.1	11.2	3.0	17.6	–	4.5	7.5	21.8	2.6	–	1.9

TABLE 1A *(concluded)*

Variable	Australia	People's Republic of China	India	Indonesia	Korea	Malaysia	New Zealand	Pakistan	Philippines	Singapore	Sri Lanka	Taiwan	Thailand
V29: Mfg. Exports	–	–	–	2.2	80.1	–	–	–	–	–	18.6	–	–
V30: Civil Liberties	1	5	2	5	5	4	1	6	5	5	3	5	3
V31: Political Rights	1	6	2	5	4	3	1	6	5	5	2	5	4
V34: Political Strikes	73	29	83	29	78	29	29	91	29	29	63	29	89
V42: Agriculture's Share GDP	6.8	–	37.4	24.8	15.8	24.1	11.3	31.1	23.2	1.4	27.6	–	25.4
V43: Industry's Share GDP	36.4	–	25.2	43.4	40.6	36.9	31.3	25.3	36.9	39.0	29.6	–	28.5
V44: Services' Share GDP	56.8	–	37.5	31.8	43.6	39.0	57.4	43.6	39.9	59.6	42.8	–	46.1

TABLE 1B
The Americas (except Canada & the USA in Table 1D)

Variable	Argentina	Brazil	Chile	Colombia	Costa Rica	El Salvador	Guatemala	Honduras	Mexico	Nicaragua	Panama	Venezuela
V1: Income	2568	2180	2378	1209	1484	647	1085	597	2040	775	1800	3841
V2: Telephone	93	30	50	64	107	19	10	8	72	22	95	58
V5: Literacy	92.6	76.1	89.0	85.2	—	57.1	—	—	82.7	57.5	87.1	76.5
V6: School	10.4	8.9	11.5	9.0	8.7	7.6	5.4	7.6	10.4	8.4	10.2	8.9
V16: Population	28.2	121	11.1	27.1	2.3	4.8	7.3	3.7	69.4	2.7	1.9	15.0
V17: GDP	72.5	264	26.4	32.7	3.3	3.1	7.9	2.2	141	2.1	3.4	57.7
V25: Foreign Property	5.1	6.5	9.4	6.5	8.2	4.9	4.8	14.2	5.8	4.4	—	9.2
V29: Mfg. Exports	21.4	32.8	8.7	19.6	26.7	34.9	23.4	12.3	—	—	8.8	—

TABLE 1B *(concluded)*

Variable	Argentina	Brazil	Chile	Colombia	Costa Rica	El Salvador	Guatemala	Honduras	Mexico	Nicaragua	Panama	Venezuela
V30: Civil Liberties	5	3	5	3	1	3	5	3	3	5	5	2
V31: Political Rights	6	4	6	2	1	1	3	6	3	5	5	1
V34: Political Strikes	87	83	73	83	73	29	63	29	80	89	73	29
V42: Agriculture's Share GDP	8.8	—	7.4	27.6	17.8	27.7	—	28.5	9.2	22.6	10.0	5.8
V43: Industry's Share GDP	37.9	—	37.6	30.7	27.0	19.8	—	26.2	34.9	31.1	21.4	47.1
V44: Services' Share GDP	53.3	—	55.0	41.7	55.2	52.5	—	45.3	55.9	46.3	68.6	47.1

TABLE 1C
Europe (except France, West Germany, Italy, and United Kingdom in Table 1D)

Variable	Bulgaria	Czechoslovakia	East Germany	Greece	Hungary	Poland	Portugal	Romania	Spain	Turkey	USSR
V1: Income	–	–	–	4007	1969	–	2351	–	5305	1353	–
V2: Telephone	141	206	189	289	118	95	138	56	315	39	89
V5: Literacy	–	–	–	84.4	98.9	98.8	71.0	–	92.6	51.3	–
V6: School	10.3	10.1	11.4	10.9	10.7	11.0	9.4	11.2	11.5	7.3	10.0
V16: Population	8.9	15.3	16.7	9.6	10.7	35.6	9.9	22.2	37.4	44.4	266
V17: GDP	–	–	–	38.6	21.1	–	23.3	–	199	60.1	–
V25: Foreign Property	–	–	–	3.3	–	–	3.1	–	3.9	0.9	–
V29: Mfg. Exports	–	–	–	41.5	–	–	68.6	–	62.4	25.9	–

TABLE 1C *(concluded)*

Variable	Bulgaria	Czechoslovakia	East Germany	Greece	Hungary	Poland	Portugal	Romania	Spain	Turkey	USSR
V30: Civil Liberties	7	7	7	2	5	5	2	6	2	3	6
V31: Political Rights	7	7	7	2	6	6	2	7	2	2	6
V34: Political Strikes	29	63	29	79	29	63	87	63	100	83	63
V42: Agriculture's Share GDP	—	—	—	17.4	—	—	12.7	—	7.1	22.7	—
V43: Industry's Share GDP	—	—	—	31.3	—	—	45.9	—	34.2	30.4	—
V44: Services' Share GDP	—	—	—	51.3	—	—	41.4	—	58.7	46.9	—

TABLE 1D
Developed Nations

Variable	Canada	France	West Germany	Italy	Japan	United Kingdom	USA
V1: Income	10757	11188	12234	6287	9063	8671	11368
V2: Telephone	686	459	464	337	460	477	788
V5: Literacy	—	—	—	93.9	—	—	99.5
V6: School	11.4	11.4	10.1	11.1	11.6	12.0	11.4
V16: Population	24.0	53.7	61.6	57.1	116.8	55.9	227.7
V17: GDP	258.6	600.9	753.1	358.1	1058.6	485.0	2588.4
V25: Foreign Property	—	—	—	—	—	—	—
V29: Mfg. Exports	—	66.7	78.5	79.0	—	—	—
V30: Civil Liberties	1	2	2	2	1	1	1
V31: Political Rights	1	1	1	2	2	1	1
V34: Political Strikes	78	97	29	87	73	93	85
V42: Agriculture's Share GDP	3.9	4.2	2.2	6.4	3.8	1.9	2.8
V43: Industry's Share GDP	33.7	35.8	47.9	42.7	42.9	34.6	34.1
V44: Services' Share GDP	62.4	60.0	49.9	50.9	53.3	63.5	63.1

CHAPTER 2

FINDING THE RIGHT SUPPLIER

- A California manufacturer of large computer systems bought monitors through its branch in Japan for nearly 40 percent less than from the manufacturer's U.S. distribution company.

- A California maker of computer peripherals bought connectors from a representative of several Taiwanese manufacturers and paid nearly three times the manufacturer's price.

- A Midwestern company selling sales promotion items negotiated fixed fees with manufacturers' representatives to develop sources and arrange for inspection and shipping of a wide variety of products.

There are three major steps to finding a good supplier offshore: (1) locating it, hopefully through an introduction, (2) determining where it is within the distribution channel, and (3) evaluating and qualifying it.

For the buyer who is just beginning to deal outside the United States, locating a supplier may be the most difficult step. The principal need in buying overseas is contacts. The buyers who remember La Guardia, Gatwick, and Haneda as the international gateways to New York, London, and Tokyo, and those whose collection of business cards gives evidence of many years of personal and business relationships abroad, are usually the ones who can most quickly locate a reasonable and reliable supplier of whatever is needed. This book can never compensate for the acquaintances built over years of international travel, for the lessons in other cultures learned from direct experience, or for the knowledge of how business in a region really works; these can only be gained from buying there.

In addition to having worked with many offshore suppliers, the experienced buyer's contacts provide a means for personal introductions to new suppliers, an important advantage in many cultures. Most buyers, and their companies, have a number of avenues that, although they won't substitute for years of offshore contacts, nevertheless offer a chance to contact a potential supplier through a personal introduction. Utilizing some of these avenues is explored later in the chapter.

Locating a supplier is only a part of a product search. Identification of the right distribution channel may be as important in the initial stage of an offshore search as finding the product itself. In the first example at the beginning of the chapter, the company avoided the overhead and profit of the manufacturer's U.S. subsidiary by buying direct from the manufacturer. The second company paid a broker to deliver goods imported from an offshore distributor, increasing its costs by the broker's commission, the distributor's profit and overhead, and additional markups on the freight and duty as well. The third was able to greatly increase its sourcing activity with little additional cost by using a company that specialized in finding and delivering quality trinkets.

International channels of distribution often carry the same names as in the United States but vary substantially in scope and function around the world. Many forms of middlemen may serve to facilitate a purchase by helping with translation, providing inspections, getting the proper documents. Others may expect a commission for little or no service or, through various devices, attempt to conceal the actual manufacturer or supplier. Some of the various forms of distribution, plus a look at their services and ranges of compensation, are reviewed under the section "International Distribution."

Neither finding a supplier with the product nor the services of a cost-effective distributor will ensure reliable quality and delivery or guarantee a relationship on which to build further business. Evaluating and qualifying an supplier is possibly the most difficult task of buying offshore. The buyer new to doing business outside the United States will again be hampered by lack of contacts—other customers of the supplier, individuals who may know something of the supplier's management, or even ordinary commercial references.

Distance itself is an impediment. A factory survey is usually reflective of a supplier's capability, work standards, and attitudes toward quality and delivery, but on-site evaluations of every prospective supplier would be prohibitive. Again, there are approaches that will partly compensate for a lack of direct information and some suggestions for developing preliminary assessments of a prospective supplier without the expense of international travel.

FINDING A SUPPLIER

The vast majority of offshore sourcing opportunities will be found in the companies that fall between the small specialty firms and the huge multinationals. Most of them are already exporting and will have some experience in working with American companies. There are a variety of ways to identify and locate them.

Consulates and Trade Boards

Matching buyers and sellers is the primary function of many consulates, especially those of countries whose national purpose seems to be exporting. Other quasi-governmental offices may also be created: "trade development boards" or "industrial promotion offices" or "chamber of commerce and trade institute and business information centers." All major exporting nations will have a promotional office of this sort as well as a consulate. They all can be found in the Yellow Pages under "Consuls" or the several variations for trade boards just listed.

The consulate's commercial attaché bears local responsibility for trade development and may administer the trade board or supplement it. The level of service will vary but most consuls can generally be expected to find at least names of major firms and their addresses and telephone numbers. At best, they will initiate a search, advising both the prospective customer and potential suppliers of a mutual interest. The offices will generate reams of literature on the companies and the industrial strength of the country it represents. Most have catalogs and directories providing an array of opportunities, plus travel and tourist information, maps, and guide books. Some may even identify a potential supplier.

Given the best level of service, inquiries may result in offers, catalogs, corporate data sheets, and customer references. The inquiry may reach the mailing lists of a half dozen advertising periodicals, the best of which may identify a source. A number of responses can be expected from distributors, manufacturer's representatives, and brokers.

The trade board may also publish promotional periodicals or know of private publications that advertise the country's exports. Many of these contain the products, names, and addresses of the manufacturers and U.S. contacts, if there are any.

Personal Contacts

Working through personal contacts is among the best ways to identify potential sources because it improves the chances of being able to directly approach a primary source without commitment to an intermediary. Personal contact may also offer early insight into the potential source's capabilities and shortcomings. It may be possible to discover what to expect in prices, terms, or other business conditions. And bona fide personal introduction is invaluable in many parts of the world.

Obtaining an introduction through a network of acquaintances increases the chances of dealing directly with a manufacturer. Leads offered by various intermediaries who will invariably hear of the search and offer services on commission should be politely deferred until every effort to make direct contact has been exhausted. Obviously, if a primary source cannot be identified, such offers can be explored; however, no obligation will have been incurred if a primary source is first found by the buyer.

Using acquaintances is probably the slowest and least manageable method of locating a primary source. It typically requires at least three introductions in a path that might include an acquaintance in a related field, to an acquaintance in the appropriate country or industry, to a contact in the appropriate industry, to the source. For at least two of the parties in this path a motive to cooperate, either for friendship or profit, will be lacking. One link in the path must by definition be international, either by mail or telephone, one slow and the other expensive. Patience, tenacity, and sometimes a little gall are required to make it work. Some incentives must be supplied, possibly lunches or incessant telephone calls, but the rewards are the lower costs of dealing direct.

Networks may be inefficient but their scope is tremendous. Big multinational banks and companies employ many expatriate Americans. A friend in any of these companies is part of a huge international network. An acquaintance sourcing offshore in a completely unrelated industry has, at least, personal contacts in the foreign business community who, in turn, will have friends in other industries. A possible last resort, and by no means a silly one for anyone with a friend living overseas, is to get the local English equivalent of the "Yellow Pages," which are published by industry groups in many countries and distributed to hotels and other places as advertising.

Professional and industry associations should be included in the network of personal acquaintances. These include not only procurement-related groups but also any in which the company's employees may participate, such as engineering associations and computer user groups. The associations themselves may have seminars related to procurement for their particular industries.

Introductions are frequently a more important part of business offshore than in the United States. It is therefore important that the first correspondence with the primary source acknowledge the intermediary who made the introduction. Acknowledgment and thanks to the intermediary is also appropriate and often useful. A note to someone who supplied an introduction may trigger a follow-up, confirming the personal nature of the relationship.

Suppliers and Customers

If they don't perceive an inquiry as threatening to their own business, suppliers can be an important part of an offshore product search. Suppliers who might be replaced would be threatened by a search, but those whose product or service is not the object of the search might be helpful. They may be sourcing offshore themselves or may be in industries that require international contacts. Even suppliers incidental to the firm's primary industry may be able to help. Their freight company, bank, or law firm may all have international contacts. Most companies with international organizations proudly present a list of the countries in which they do business in their annual report and most provide addresses and telephone numbers as well. With an introduction from the local office, the offshore branch may expend at least a few minutes at the task out of courtesy for a customer of the corporation.

A firm's customers are equally good prospects. They won't see a search as threatening and they offer as great a potential for good contacts as a supplier. Any firm that sells overseas will have good international contacts.

Trade Shows

Many foreign firms are represented in the hundreds of national and international trade shows and expositions. Normally the whole spectrum of sources is represented—distributors, manufacturers' representatives, the U.S. subsidiaries of foreign firms, and some of the actual manufacturers. If the booth doesn't indicate which, a business card probably will. Very often, the small manufacturer is found in the smaller, less-expensive booths of the trade shows and may go unnoticed amid the spectacle of the large companies.

Manufacturers with many products may exhibit at a wide range of shows. A company in ceramics may exhibit tableware at a home show and high-temperature crucibles at an industrial exhibit. A foundry may offer winches and cleats at a boat show but power supply heat sinks at an electronics fair. Distributors and manufacturers' representatives are often willing to divulge their sources if the product being sought is not one that they would market. The marine hardware distributor at a boat show, for example, might identify the foundry that makes its cleats to someone interested in buying industrial castings. Even if the foundry is not interested, an inquiry could produce a recommendation to another foundry that might be.

At any trade exhibition, showpiece products will be on display, an initial characterization of the firm's capability, technology, and workmanship. If the firm is seeking contract work, it may also profile its organization, facility, and equipment. The promotional material distributed at shows frequently includes the primary source's name, address, and telephone number.

Contract Searches

A contract search is any request to an intermediary to locate a product or source offshore. It should be the last resort of an offshore product search. Although there may be very good reasons to employ a distributor or manufacturer's representative later, there is considerable negotiating leverage in having first identified the primary offshore source. Knowing the primary source is the principal leverage of an intermediary. If an offshore product search has identified a source, an intermediary will be forced to justify the commission on the value of services to be provided, not on having found the source. Nevertheless, contract searches are sometimes necessary. Attempts at locating a primary source may have been unproductive or identified only marginal prospects, or urgency may dictate using as many approaches to a search as possible.

A contract search should be an agreement to pay a commission upon the purchase of a product, not for having identified a potential source, with both the manufacturer and the product subject to the buyer's approval. The search should not be authorized until all the intermediary's services, not merely locating the source, have been discussed and a fee schedule established for them. Many companies, especially independent brokers, adjust their fees to reflect their scope of participation in a transaction. For simply locating a source a *finder's fee* might be a small percentage of the sale. A hefty commission would be expected for substantial participation in the transaction and importation of the product. Commissions are generally negotiable and will vary widely even within an industry. A company with more business than it can handle might quote a much larger commission than would another, hungrier firm.

The search agreement should also address the future relationship with the intermediary. An intermediary will expect that all subsequent business with the primary source will go through it, and for the same commission. If the intermediary is employed simply to locate the source, limit any obligation to the product being sought, reserving the right to buy other products direct, without commission. Limit the commissions to a finder's fee, payable on purchases only for a fixed period. If significant other services are expected from the intermediary and purchases from the primary source may eventually result in disproportional compensation, the agreement should anticipate amending the commission structure. A sliding scale might be appropriate, or the agreement may be reviewed annually. Finally, provision should be made to dismiss the intermediary if its performance proves unacceptable, even if the primary source is performing well.

INTERNATIONAL DISTRIBUTION

Buying direct from the manufacturer is usually the least expensive but it may not be the best way to buy offshore, and it may not even be possible. Some form of intermediary, or middleman, may be required to effect a transaction and, even if none is required, many intermediaries may be encountered during a search. Primary manufacturers are least likely to turn up early in a search. It is more likely that one of several possible intermediaries will be the first to respond to a search, hoping for a share of the business.

The terms used for the various forms of distribution offshore differ little from those that will be encountered in the United States, and anyone familiar with channel structure in the United States already understands the services each may be expected to provide. Internationally, however, differences in local business practice, available capital, expected margins, or the depth of the distribution system may result in services or expectations that differ substantially from what would be expected in the United

States. It is almost imperative for the buyer to be aware of distribution alternatives before attempting to locate a product.

Asking an intermediary to find a product generally implies a commitment to pay for that service, adding to the cost of buying "factory direct." Having sourced one product from a manufacturer, an intermediary expects commissions on future business from the same manufacturer. Without first understanding the precise role a middleman will play in a transaction, a buyer could inadvertently pay a 15 percent search commission to some U.S. company to buy from a foreign distributor whose allegiance is to the manufacturing source. The U.S. firm might not be capable of providing the support needed, and the foreign distributor would have no obligation or incentive to do so. Such a situation may be unavoidable, but this chapter will at least explain how to recognize and possibly avoid the predicament.

On the other hand, an intermediary may be required to handle the many tasks of arranging for importation, to help bridge a language barrier, or even to manage a contract after an agreement has been reached. Many would consider a 5 percent commission adequate compensation for finding a product, studying its specifications and helping to interpret them to the manufacturer, performing source inspections, keeping the buyer informed about the manufacturer's progress or problems, making all the arrangements for shipping, and even making hotel reservations and meeting clients at the airport when they visit the source. Such service may be far more economical than handling all these details within the buyer's company.

INTERMEDIARIES OR MIDDLEMEN

Any potential source will fall into one of two broad categories: the primary suppliers of product or services and intermediaries, or *middlemen*. Middlemen also fall into distinct categories: (1) *distributors*, who buy and resell a primary source's product and make a profit by marking up the price, (2) *manufacturers' representatives*, who market a primary source's product for a commission, and (3) *brokers*, who act as intermediaries between buyer and seller without necessarily having had a relationship with the primary source before arranging the sale. Other intermediaries, trading companies and independent agents for example, may act as all three, distributing for some manufacturers, representing others, and brokering any business they can. The distinctions are important in determining who will be responsible to meet schedules, to whom defective product will be returned, and who will be paid for the product.

Distributors

Distributors are characterized by buying and reselling within a designated territory for a primary source. They normally accept customer orders and receive payment, relieving the primary manufacturer of the receivables risk. The distributor's profit is generated by marking up the price of the goods or, alternatively, by buying at a discount from the primary source. A distributor may accept after-sale responsibility for the goods, repairing or replacing defective products, or provide service and customer training.

In the United States, distributors regularly hold an inventory for immediate delivery to their customers and have contractually protected, exclusive territories. Both industrial and retail distribution networks tend to be shallow, that is, there are few intermediaries between the source and customer. In many industries, U.S. distributors provide substantial customer training and support and bear warranty and repair responsibility.

Internationally, especially in undercapitalized economies, the distributor's role may be substantially different: The characteristic buying and reselling of the primary manufacturer's goods remains the same, but the function is often little more than that of a receivables buffer for the primary manufacturer. The distributor will maintain a sales force but little stock, especially in areas of limited capital. The distributor's sales representatives often work closely with the primary manufacturer and quote delivery as a function of production lead times. The product may be shipped directly from manufacturer to customer even though the order was taken by the distributor.

As in the United States, offshore distributors normally have exclusive sales rights to a territory, either geographically or by customer base, but the territory may be substantially smaller or the customer base narrower. Exclusivity in the United States normally precludes sales by the primary source. Offshore, many manufacturers retain some rights to make direct sales, especially those for export. A few distributors may also have the right to export or, at least, deliver to a foreign buyer's freight forwarder.

In much of the world, distribution systems tend to be far more complex than in the United States, due partly to capital restraints and partly to historical factors. The effects of limited capital on distributor size are readily understandable: Numerous territories, or a deep hierarchy of distributors within a territory, spread the inventory and receivables investment over a greater number of companies, requiring less individual capital from each. At the same time, limited capital may also limit the number of products, or product lines, an individual distributor can carry. In capital-poor areas, such as Latin America, many distributors therefore carry a very limited line, sometimes only one, or may compete with several other distributors of the same line because none of them are large enough to secure exclusive distribution rights from a manufacturer.

In Asia, limited capital still influences distribution patterns in the newly industrializing countries, and complex systems persist in Japan, Korea, and Taiwan as well. Japan's distribution is probably the most complex system anywhere and is unlikely to change. A typical distribution chain may flow from the manufacturer to any of several "house" distributors, regional distributors, local distributors, subdistributors, local "principal" retailers, and, often, subretailers. The last don't even carry stock but will "have one for you tomorrow" and pick one up from the local principal retailers. A commodity shortage reveals the depth of such a distribution hierarchy.

> In the early 1970s, Japanese papers ran an article that newsprint was expected to be in short supply worldwide owing to the coincidence of overhauls and resultant down-time of a number of mills.
>
> Japanese housewives are hoarders of almost everything, a habit left over from the deprivation after the war. Not paying attention to what kind of paper the article referred to, or perhaps erroneously extrapolating, Tokyo housewives stripped the city of toilet

paper. Hoarding purchases were repeated all over Japan. Supplies in the pipeline were gone in days. Newspapers reported that stores, distributors, and manufacturers were out of stock throughout the country. Hotel chains weathered the first few days by chartering planeloads from the United States.

When new production finally returned to store shelves, it gathered dust. It was later estimated that the distribution pipeline had almost a month's supply in it, for a country of 120 million people!

It is often necessary, and occasionally advantageous, to source through an offshore distributor. Many primary sources may sell exclusively through one or several distributors, depending entirely on them for their sales and marketing functions. In such cases, they build only to order and simply won't have the capability to administer the sale. Many, with little or no international experience, may wish to rely on a distributor to negotiate for them and to implement the subsequent agreement. Principals of a primary source may not speak English and, to avoid any embarrassment, will accept international business only through their distributor. In all such cases primary sources will recommend or introduce a client to their distributors. Although employees of the primary source may thereafter be in attendance during negotiations, distributors will act on their behalf.

Procurement may also be facilitated by a distributor if the primary source does not have sufficient English-speaking staff to interpret specifications or respond adequately to communications. A large distributor that handles products from many small manufacturers may be able to offer better credit terms and provide more reliable warranty repair or other services than the primary source.

Whenever circumstances or opportunity indicates the use of a distributor when sourcing offshore, every effort should be made to identify a primary distributor before making an inquiry. Buying from a subdistributor implies that profit and overhead have been added to the cost of the goods at least three times— by the manufacturer, the primary distributor, and the secondary distributor. It also means that product defects will be handled at least two steps from the organization that can correct them. Because subdistribution contracts are usually very limited, it is likely that any international inquiry will be directed to a main distributor anyway, but, having first recorded the contact, they may be entitled to a commission, adding to the cost of the product.

Manufacturers' Representatives

A manufacturer's representative does not buy and resell the manufacturer's product but sells on commission. Depending on the arrangements between the manufacturer and the representative, orders may be issued to either one, but shipments and invoices will issue from the manufacturer to the customer. A manufacturer's representative does not accept the credit risk of a sale.

In the United States, manufacturers' representatives generally have exclusive distribution rights. As they sell on commission, few are willing to represent a manufacturer's product line with a competitor in the same territory. The customer pays the manufacturer a price that includes the representative's commission, which is then paid to the representative. The commissions are based on sales volume or some other formula agreed on between the manufacturer and the representative.

Generally, manufacturers' representatives in the United States sell only for manufacturers with whom they have contractual arrangements. They are usually well trained to present both the products and the manufacturers. Well-established manufacturers' representatives market for a number of manufacturers. In the United States a representative who asks "If I can find it, will you buy it?" is apt to be a marginal supplier, either too new to have secured representation of many manufacturers or one with whom manufacturers are unwilling to do business.

Internationally, it is not uncommon for many companies, including primary manufacturers, to represent other firms and products. The products offer additional business opportunity but their representation may actually be little more than brokering occasional sales. The representative's relationship with the manufacturer may be tenuous, often little more than acquaintance. Compensation for the sale may be agreed on during the negotiations. Not infrequently, a representative will offer to find the "exact part" needed for "only a 15-percent commission," whereas many organizations would offer much more service, plus the part, at far lower cost.

Between these two extremes lie a wide range of opportunities for offshore sourcing. Many small firms that represent foreign manufacturers offer a wide range of services and have established extensive contacts for a variety of products. Most operate within niche markets and have already located sources for the commodity within the niche. Specialized to this degree, they are generally knowledgeable about commodity specifications, prevailing prices, and market availability or lead times. They may have established freight and customs broker relationships. The well-established or better-capitalized firms may also be willing to accept order and delivery responsibility, normally the functions of a distributor.

To the small firm first exploring offshore sourcing, such a representative may offer the quickest way to the savings of going offshore. Identifying a prospective source is greatly simplified. Other U.S. companies will have bought through both the representative and the suppliers serviced by the representative and can supply references for both. Many details of shipping and importing will have been worked out. Because the representative does not carry the receivables, is not responsible for product defects or support, and does not have the overhead of a distributor, its profit margin on the sale will be slimmer than a distributor's. The purchase, however, will usually be in foreign currency, entailing a foreign exchange risk, and the initial terms will probably be on letter of credit. Because of the limited role of manufacturers' representatives in a transaction, the many issues of support, warranty, repair or return, and product credits should be confirmed with the primary source.

Unlike offshore distributors, manufacturers' representatives may be based either in the United States or overseas. Although it should be apparent that buying from a United States distributor isn't sourcing offshore, the location of a manufacturer's representative is almost irrelevant to a purchase. In fact, if the representative is in the U.S., the buyer benefits from cheap and easy communications.

Brokers

Brokers' profits are derived from fees for bringing two parties to a transaction together. In practice, industrial brokers may also perform a wide range of tasks that vary depending on the individual transaction. At times, therefore, the broker may appear in the role of distributor, buying and reselling to the customer, or as a representative, selling on commission. However, unlike a distributor or manufacturer's representative, the relationship between a broker and primary source is transaction dependent. Brokers may therefore seek fees from either the buyer or seller in a transaction and sometimes from both.

Because brokers must negotiate a fee, or commission, for each transaction, they will focus selling effort on a product, obtaining the buyer's agreement before disclosing the source. Having arranged a transaction, brokers expect similar fees for subsequent purchases from the same source. It is therefore important for the buying client to have established a clear understanding of both the fees and services expected of the broker, for both the initial and subsequent purchases, even before starting an evaluation of the product offering.

Brokers have no territorial limitations except for any that may be imposed by their own business licenses or charters. It is therefore possible for them to act as intermediaries to a transaction even in the "exclusive" territories of distributors or manufacturers' representatives. If, for example, a U.S. distributor has exclusive rights to sell a product, the broker can arrange for a sale to take place elsewhere, directly from the source or from another, offshore, intermediary.

An experienced broker with extensive contacts in an industry can greatly reduce the search time for a new product and can be very helpful in arranging introductions, assisting in communications with the primary source, and in many of the commercial transactions of importing. With an established fee and service agreement mutually beneficial to both broker and buying client, many small companies can develop an offshore sourcing program even with very limited time and staffing.

Agents and *Agents*

Agent and *agency* are tightly defined by U.S. law and refer to a relationship wherein an individual or corporation acting as agent for another, the *principal*, has the authority to make commitments on behalf of the principal. Internationally, the terms are often used with little regard to the actual relationship between agent and principal. In many cases, international *agents* are often brokers to whom no principal has delegated any authority or given any power of attorney but who may, nevertheless, be recognized as possibly facilitating a sale. A business card announcing "Agents for (some well-known company)," especially if it uses the company's logo, probably reflects a relationship similar to the U.S. definition but as defined by local law. An individual who simply calls her- or himself an agent could be almost anything.

A rapidly growing electronics firm, eager to take advantage of the low building costs, labor rates, and large labor pool in one of the newly industrialized countries of southest Asia, purchased an uncompleted building in a new industrial park. The start-up team quickly learned why the building was sold still unfinished; the previous owner apparently had not learned how to "grease" the system so that it worked smoothly for him.

The first obstacle to starting production was a lack of electricity. The industrial park was scheduled to receive additional power but, as in many countries with limited resources for infrastructure development, determining exactly when the substations would be built proved difficult. After meetings with successively more important positions in the government, the team members reached the ministerial level of the energy hierarchy. They were told that the government could not guarantee power any time soon but would recommend an agent or consultant to help develop the necessary applications for a private substation on the property. Although the cost of an electrical substation had never been considered in the plans for the factory, the company managed to secure power, the country got a tax-free boost to its electrical distribution system, the agent received a healthy fee, and many people involved in reviewing plans and issuing permits for private substations probably received gratuities (from the agent) for their help in expediting the process.

Later, during several of the remaining stages of construction, government or local inspectors raised serious objections to the ventilation, fire safety, and other issues related to the interpretation of building or business codes. Virtually all of the interpretations seemed to involve prohibitively expensive solutions and almost any of them could have killed the project. Finally, one of the inspectors recommended that the start-up team consider retaining a consultant to help develop a solution to a particular problem and enlightenment dawned on the team. Since then, the company's factory management has become fairly adept at distinguishing between real, negotiable, problems and those which require the services of one of the many "agents" who can facilitate the solution of difficult local problems.

Payments to expedite, encourage, or ensure the performance of a legal task are not considered bribery by the U.S. but "facilitating payments." Such payments may be both common and necessary in areas where minor positions of authority receive only meager salaries and whose holders are expected to supplement their incomes in other ways. Such activity is still widespread in many areas, especially in newly industrialized countries of Asia and should probably be anticipated in some of the recovering nations of Eastern Europe. It appears to have greatly diminished in countries determined to become major economic players. Malaysia, for example, emulating its stern but successful neighbor, Singapore, has largely eliminated this behavior.

Trading Companies

Many international firms may distribute for some manufacturers, represent others, and broker still other transactions, but there is a class of companies that has institutionalized the role of intermediary in international commerce: the trading company. Until a few decades ago Jardine-Mathieson, Swire, and other well-known British and American companies were the dominant traders. More recently the Japanese have dominated trading, and now blanket the world with their activities. Although their grain and lumber businesses suffered severe losses in the 1970s, the scope of the traders' activity can be seen in these enterprises. The trading companies themselves often owned the distribution system from grain elevators, river barges and dock facilities, deep-draft ships, harbor and loading facilities, all the way to the mills themselves. Their present depth and breadth are unknown elsewhere; if there is a market of significant proportions, they will trade in it.

Trading companies may distribute, domestically or internationally, for a number of companies, may represent many more, broker other transactions, or even manage large projects and create vast industries on their own. Their assets, of course, include innumerable contacts; if the profit opportunity is great enough, they will trade, source, or develop whatever a customer needs. Because of their global presence, language is rarely a problem and they can offer a range of skills smaller companies can't match. If the opportunity warrants, they can provide technical, financial, marketing, and other services in almost any area of a client's business.

Unless elements of the trading company's size or scope offer distinct benefits to a transaction, however, it may not offer a client any more than another, smaller intermediary. Because of their size and complexity, trading companies' prices may be higher than those of a smaller firm with less overhead to support. Unless they have exclusive distribution rights for a product, for example, or are needed to implement large transactions that smaller companies cannot handle, sourcing through them offers few advantages over any other offshore source.

Costs and Risks of Using Intermediaries

To the primary source, the costs of selling through an intermediary are generally in proportion to the services provided. A distributorship that bears the burdens of advertising and warranty repair service, for example, will expect greater compensation for its part in a sale than a distributor that does little more than accept orders and carry the receivables risk. Similarly, because they do carry the risks of principals in a transaction, distributors receive a greater share of the profit in a transaction than manufacturers' representatives receive. If no other services are provided, a broker's fee for introducing the parties to a transaction should make them the least-expensive form of intermediary.

This relationship is relative and varies by product, among industries, and from country to country. Distributors that bear the major burden of a product's marketing and sales effort, advertising and promotion, transportation, and selling costs, plus the credit and inventory risks will receive most of the value of a sale. In some countries and some industries this may amount to 60 percent to 80 percent of the product price. Conversely, many distributors receive only 15 percent to 20 percent for delivering orders for a large manufacturer that directs and funds its own product's marketing program. The costs of using manufacturers' representatives and brokers will also vary widely depending on the product or industry, the services provided, and competitive pressure.

The risks of using an intermediary are generally less when (1) a strong relationship exists between a primary source and the intermediary and (2) the intermediary assumes significant responsibilities for a transaction. Although the rule is not always true, these criteria usually mean the most-expensive forms of intermediary should result in the least risk. When applied to the basic forms just described, these criteria imply that a distributor will offer the least risk, a broker the most. Figure 2.1 summarizes the advantages and disadvantages of various sourcing intermediaries.

A well-established relationship reduces the possibility of miscommunication between the intermediary and primary source. Better communication can be expected between a primary source and one of its distributors or representatives than with a broker with which it has never done business. Fewer misunderstandings will occur about which party, the primary source or the intermediary, will be responsible for various aspects of a transaction; which must arrange transportation; which must obtain customer approvals for changes in specifications or delivery; or which will communicate problems.

The responsibilities of an intermediary are reflected in its costs. A distributor, in purchasing and reselling products and accepting both payment and the risk of nonpayment, will have

Figure 2–1

Advantages and Disadvantages of Various Forms of International Distribution Channels

Source Intermediaries or "Middlemen"	Advantages	Disadvantages
Distributors Buy and resell goods. Accept orders and payment. Assume warranty responsibility. May offer customer training.	Handle cultural, commercial, and technical problems. If delivery in U.S., payment in dollars, standard terms. Simple handling of product defects.	Among the most costly sources: buyer pays both manufacturer's and distributor's profit and overhead. Probably foreign currency, L/C terms.
Manufacturers' Representatives Accept orders on behalf of a source, paid commission for the service. May provide technical and commercial support.	Handle cultural, commercial, and technical problems. Generally less expensive to use than a distributor.	Payment in foreign currency. L/C terms if a foreign rep. company. Bears no warranty liability, little use in dealing with defects.
Brokers Bring parties to a transaction together for a fee. Services vary widely.	Least expensive intermediary Wide range of services possible. May have wide contacts in the industry. Most negotiable.	Least responsible for source or product performance, warranty. Probably little technical support. Foreign currency, L/C terms probable.
Trading Companies Broad scope of activities from brokering, representation, distribution, program management.	Worldwide contacts, broadest scope of sources. Experience and capability. Few cultural or language problems.	Generally a costly alternative. Most prefer to trade in existing markets, or make a market for new product, not to deal in isolated inquiries. Because of their scale, most buyers have little leverage.

Primary Sources

Large Multinationals The majority of international business. May prefer new customers to buy through distribution or U.S. subsidiaries, which cannot be considered an offshore source.	Undisputed capability, possible benefits of economies of scale. Good support, training, warranty performance. Few cultural or language impediments.	Because of scale, few buyers have negotiating leverage. No benefit in purchases through U.S. subsidiary.
Midsize Manufacturers The vast majority of source opportunities. Public or private. Most already exporting. May have a U.S. presence in a *liaison office*.	Low costs at acceptable levels of risk. Opportunities for close, long-term relationships.	Some cultural and language barriers to overcome. Foreign currency, letter of credit.
Small Specialty Firms Usually individually or privately owned. Limited capability; usually one process or service.	Lowest cost. Probably most personalized, attentive service.	Most likely to present cultural, language problems. Buyer responsible for freight, duty of transaction. Foreign currency, letter of credit.
Captives Wholly owned subsidiaries or subcontractors controlled by larger firms through investment or predatory purchasing.	If accessible, may be very inexpensive and accustomed to quality, on-time performance.	Normally unwilling or precluded from accepting direct orders. Extra cost if accessed through the dominant company.

the greater costs and a larger responsibility for a sale than either a manufacturer's representative or a broker. Conversely, a broker accepts the least responsibility and, presumably, costs the least.

PRIMARY SOURCES

Direct purchase from a primary source is almost invariably less expensive than procurement through any form of intermediary. Although both buyer and seller assume much greater responsibilities, the benefits frequently outweigh the effort required. The communication delays inherent in multiparty transactions are gone, making scheduling and rescheduling easier. Changes are more easily communicated, especially as a manufacturer is more likely to be familiar with the product and manufacturing processes and problems, than any middleman to a transaction.

Primary sources should always be the target of an offshore product search even if it is later decided to purchase through an intermediary. When primary sources can be located without prior commitment to an intermediary, and when their own contractual arrangements don't preclude direct sales, the ability to make such a decision is often an advantage during subsequent negotiations. Small companies, with a limited ability to administer the additional work entailed, may wish to focus their direct purchases to a few important products and use intermediaries for many, less-expensive ones. Where resource and communication problems are not limitations, direct purchase is normally the object of an offshore procurement program.

During an offshore product search two characteristics of the primary source are of particular interest: (1) its size and (2) its presence in the United States, if any. When measured by these criteria, two extremes emerge: the United States subsidiaries of large foreign companies and very small, often family-owned, manufacturers with no visibility in the United States.

Offshore Multinationals

At the upper end of the scale are many companies that may not want to sell directly to new customers. The very large firms overseas can, and will, provide all the services a buyer needs. Some may do so only for a company that is already an important customer and with whom they already have a long relationship. These companies are already well known because of their massive presence in world markets. Many of these companies, and particularly those in Asia like Japan's Mitsubishi or Korea's Samsung, operate on much slimmer profit margins than an American firm would consider acceptable. To ensure against loss, they prefer to sell through distributors who accept the credit risks, handle the account, and make a distributor's markup. Until a customer demonstrates that its credit is good, purchases are at a consistently high volume, and exerts so much price pressure that the big company can't afford to pay the distributor and keep the account, the very large firms probably won't sell direct.

The progression to becoming a Japanese company's house account can be maddeningly slow and controlled. Some years ago a division of Singer was doing business with Hitachi. At first, all the business was through Hitachi America, the U.S. subsidiary. The market was changing rapidly and Singer was often discussing the phaseout of one item, phasing in a second, and planning for a third. The Singer division began to get visits from the international sales manager and the general manager of the Hitachi plant making the goods. Several divisional executives and the divisional president began to visit Hitachi once or twice a year. The director of the Hitachi division became a regular visitor to the United States; his boss, the group managing director, almost as often. After five or six years, Hitachi was the sole source of one of Singer's product lines. The business was very profitable for both.

After several years of buying direct, in yen, at a level around $10 million per year, Singer was approached by one of Hitachi's competitors for a license to one of Singer's products. Hitachi was equally interested. Singer and Hitachi embarked on discussion to form a joint venture company in Japan.

After months of discussion and numerous trips back and forth to Tokyo by Singer and Hitachi staff, executives, and lawyers, Singer thought it had an agreement and was ready to fund the new company. Nothing happened. The local Hitachi people dropped in a few times. Singer politely inquired if there were problems, whether discussions should be resumed to review something unclear. Nothing.

A Singer staff member finally called a young Japanese in the local office with whom he had a close enough personal relationship to ask for some enlightenment. The young Japanese said, "Of course our Board of Directors must meet to decide if Hitachi wants a long-term relationship with Singer."

U.S. Subsidiaries of Foreign Companies

The big companies generally have United States subsidiaries. For the most part they are wholly owned, incorporated in the United States, and have exclusive distribution rights for the manufacturer's products in the United States. For the largest of the multinational companies, subsidiaries market and support products from the parent company's plants all over the world and possibly U.S. plants as well. Smaller firms may have U.S. subsidiaries that import and export but do not offer direct sales and support, marketing instead through national or regional distributors. In either case, because of their exclusivity, purchases from the primary manufacturer cannot be made in the United States without the added cost and profit of the subsidiary, and sometimes those of a distributor.

It is possible to avoid these added costs by purchasing through the buyer's own offshore subsidiary, if one exists and if its charter permits. In the United States, custom, aided by the force of law in some situations, leads to fairly uniform offerings to all buyers. In most of the rest of the world, however, substantial discounts may be available to entice buyers or freeze out competition. The possible savings of buying through a buyer's offshore subsidiary is often worth the effort of arranging for a local purchase to avoid the markups, currency hedging, and intracompany profit costs of the manufacturer's U.S. subsidiary. Other benefits accrue to subsidiary buying. The subsidiary can make the transaction in the local language; will arrange for payment in local currency; can ensure that specifications, packaging, freight, and delivery requirements are understood; and can expedite locally when troubles arise. With only a little planning, the deliveries can be made directly to a freight forwarder. The subsidiary need never see or handle the product.

A word of caution is appropriate: Most countries object to the notion of "exporting profit." In the preceding situation, the foreign subsidiary will have provided a service that would normally require compensation and, therefore, taxable revenue. When sourcing offshore through a subsidiary, it should be paid a small compensation for the cost of the service and a reasonable profit for the service.

Small Specialty Firms

At the small end of the scale of offshore manufacturers are small firms, usually privately or even family owned, that specialize in a single industry. Communication with them may be difficult; few have sales staffs prepared to operate in international markets. Nevertheless, finding one is often very rewarding. Because of their small size, limited sales, low marketing overhead, and their frequent eagerness to participate in an international market, their prices are generally low. Monitoring their performance may require additional expense, and independent inspection of their products may be advisable and will probably be welcomed. It may even be necessary to hire an independent company to monitor a small manufacturer. Services such as inspections, schedule confirmation, assistance in documentation, and drawing review usually cost less than an intermediary's commissions.

The relationship between buyer and seller should be closely examined if the offshore source is a very small company. Too often, in the excitement of entering the international arena, a small company may underbid the sale or overcommit its resources. To the buyer, the arrangement will appear to be ideal: low prices and very personalized service. Such a situation can sour quickly if the source finds it is losing money, if the buyer's needs grow faster than the source can expand, or if problems or delays tax the source's limited resources. Many companies try to limit any one customer to no more than 20 percent of their business to ensure against predatory pricing or the impact of losing the account. When sourcing from a very small company the buyer should take some responsibility for assuring that the relationship is in scale.

Midsize Manufacturers

The majority of opportunities will be found between the extremes of the multinational firms and the small, family-owned shops. Companies of this size offer the best combination of reliability and reasonable price to an offshore procurement program. They do not carry the costs of an international distribution system and cannot charge the premium of an international reputation. They are nevertheless mature firms and will have the experience, skills, and equipment needed to compete in their industry.

Many will have previously exported and may be marketing in the United States through distributors or representative in the United States. They often have branch offices in the United States to import or provide marketing support. Very often they have only one branch, normally close to the nearest large U.S. port of entry. South American company branches, therefore, most likely would be found in Miami or San Diego; those of European companies near Boston, New York, or Philadelphia; and the Asian firms in Los Angeles, San Francisco, and Seattle. Midsize manufacturers will generally have both experience in exporting and a staff with the language and other skills needed to accept direct orders.

Liaison Offices

Offshore manufacturers too small to establish their own subsidiaries in the United States may create *liaison offices*. The United States permits the establishment of these to facilitate sales to the United States but severely limits their scope of activity. Liaison offices need not be incorporated here, but neither can they accept orders or payment, own goods for sale, or otherwise participate in a sale. In short, they will carry no liability in a transaction but are restricted to providing assistance to the primary source and its U.S. customers. Liaison offices are staffed with employees of the offshore parent and negotiation with them is effectively the same as with the parent. Short of actually going abroad, it is as close a contact as can be made to an offshore source.

A manufacturer with a U.S. liaison office may be an ideal partner for a small company just beginning an offshore sourcing program. The fact that the manufacturer has a liaison office indicates that it is interested in exporting, yet it is too small to dictate terms in the same way the large companies can. The presence of a liaison office also demonstrates an English language capability and a degree of familiarity with international business.

Captive Sources

There is a group of companies that may not want to do business directly—the captives. Many larger companies have such a dominant position with their suppliers that the latter will often refer a buyer to the larger company to buy its products. This response should be expected from a small manufacturer that is a wholly owned subsidiary of a big firm, but it will also be encountered where such a relationship is not clear. The large firm may be a minority stockholder, having helped fund the smaller company. Similarly, funding may have been provided by the larger firm's bank, supported by the large firm's orders as a form of collateral. Very often, the captive relationship grew from simple predatory buying practices on the part of the larger company. At any rate, the smaller company will have abandoned much of its direct market to the larger company, in exchange for which the major firm handles the selling of its supplier's sales.

Captive source products are normally available only through the parent, or dominant, company and will include the added costs of the dominant company's administration and profit. Occasionally, however, excess capacity or other factors may make a captive accessible to an outside buyer, creating an excellent opportunity for offshore sourcing. Because of its relationship with the dominant company, the captive's prices are generally favorable and it will be accustomed to producing quality products and delivering on time. Direct purchase from a captive company, though, will always carry a risk. As a captive, its production capacity may be preempted by the dominant company, slowing or stopping production for any other customers.

SUPPLIER QUALIFICATION

Problems that are a nuisance with a U.S. supplier can take on monumental proportions when sourcing offshore. A production delay, which forces the use of air instead of sea freight to meet a customer demand, could absorb all the profit on a sale. No matter who pays for them, freight cost triples if goods are returned for repair. Travel costs preclude too many on-site visits for engineering or manufacturing support. Even communication costs increase dramatically when problems arise.

Supplier qualification is an essential part of an offshore sourcing program. The cost of a survey is small compared to the costs of doing business with a poor supplier. Companies not in the practice of supplier qualification should start a program before attempting to source offshore. Those that already have such a program should review the situations that may occur outside the United States: inadequate power and other utilities, limited communications, poor transportation facilities, or political and social conditions that may detrimentally affect procurement.

The qualifications of an offshore source can be structured as a series of tests, each designed to eliminate unsuitable suppliers before the expense of the next test is incurred. A factory survey, which implies the expense of foreign travel, should be the last. Ideally, the survey can be a confirmation of information gathered earlier and can be scheduled to coincide with the start of negotiations. The same tests provide criteria to choose among several suppliers. Beginning with the source's response to an inquiry, qualification might proceed as follows:

1. Initial Response
2. Supplier Profile
3. Reference and Credit Checks
4. Location and Infrastructure
5. Plant Survey

The Initial Response

Although an initial response won't prove a supplier qualified, it provides the earliest opportunity to disqualify one. The effort that would be needed to turn a poor supplier into a good one offshore will be better spent continuing the product search. If the response isn't both eager for the business and indicative of the ability to deliver it, file it as a last resort. Some cultures avoid making stark negative responses. If the answer is not affirmative, or does not include a request for more information, it is probably a "no bid."

The cover letter of a good, positive indication of a match will specifically address the equipment, experience, past performance, and current products that fit the stated requirements. The corporate literature will have photographs of the equipment needed and sales brochures will show similar products. Information provided may include samples of products being made for another customer, even, perhaps, customer references. Public companies may include annual reports, often in the foreign language if the company is not known internationally. Sometimes quotations may be included subject to confirmation of specifications.

The response may offer interesting subjective insights. The cover letter may be difficult to understand, but proofreading and presentation of the written information is an indication of the attention given to quality. A supplier who is confident of meeting the requirements, or reasonably certain of enough to keep the discussions going, will also subtly begin the negotiation process.

Avoid Negotiating

Each step in a qualification program will increase the supplier's expectations of doing business. Almost invariably a supplier will attempt to escalate the program to other business discussions. Nevertheless, negotiations should be avoided throughout the supplier qualification process, just as the initial inquiry to the potential source should avoid stating target prices or volumes. Much of the information needed to qualify a supplier may be useful during negotiations. In particular, the last test, the plant survey, is an opportunity to see if the source is operating at full capacity or needs more work to reach capacity or to utilize idle equipment. Delay also allows time to collect other sources' quotes before negotiating with any of them.

Escalation of the qualification process, and the subsequent

timing of negotiations, can be controlled by the release of information. The request for a supplier profile may include enough information to keep the supplier's attention but may be insufficient to prepare a quotation. A Request for Quotation (RFQ) might accompany the supplier survey questionnaire. Therefore, if the initial response includes them, ignore any quotes. If the response contains a quote, it was developed with inadequate information or is preemptory, an attempt to establish a high price at the start of negotiations. The same applies to other terms and conditions that might be stated, such as payment terms, delivery point, or warranty period.

Supplier Profile

A supplier profile is a more specific request for information about a potential source. It may not be needed if the initial response was comprehensive or the source is a well-known company, but collecting supplier profiles is often helpful to companies that source a wide variety of products offshore. The questions should be fairly brief and clearly differentiated from a survey, which includes a lengthy questionnaire. Again, a profile cannot serve to qualify a supplier but will help avoid the travel, cost, and effort of surveying an unqualified one.

Some of the questions may not be answered. Large, public companies may simply supply an annual report in response. Small, private companies may refuse to provide detailed financial information. For the majority of companies in between, however, the answers can be very useful and revealing. A sample supplier profile request is included in Appendix 2. Its final request is to provide authorization for reference checks.

Reference and Credit Check

Credit
If possible, the bank references should be followed up through the buyer's own bank. It may be more familiar with local practice and can make a more appropriate inquiry in the situation. Dun & Bradstreet will also do a credit check on an international company. Its fees for one are much higher than for a U.S. credit

check, however, several hundred dollars or more, and the information provided is frequently skimpy.

Credit and banking information about a potential source should not be weighed by the same criteria as in the United States. Because of the differences in business practice, information may be misleading unless local practices are understood. Debt-to-equity ratios that would be viewed with apprehension in the United States would be conservative in Japan or Israel. In many areas, financing a business on payables is common practice. A supplier whose payables average over 60, or even 90, days is not necessarily in financial difficulty. It may even be using its financial resources less efficiently than the local norm. An implication that questions the company's financial stability should, of course, be cause for concern.

Either a bank reference or Dun & Bradstreet report may indicate whether a supplier is factoring its receivables and, possibly, to what degree. Factoring, or selling receivables to a bank at a substantial discount before they are due, is common practice in many places and should not necessarily be regarded disparagingly. It does indicate that a supplier will accept payment on open account but may also indicate that setting off debits may be difficult.

Customers

Most companies proudly list big-name customers and will supply customer lists when requested. Request for specific references will normally result in a list reduced to those most likely to report favorably, but such references are among the few sources of independent information available to a buyer.

Ex-customers are possibly the best source of information about a potential source. Their comments or observations about a supplier will not be clouded by a current relationship. Prior customers who moved because of changes in the supplier's or their own business may have been quite happy with the relationship and provide useful suggestions and insights. Those who took their business elsewhere because of quality, price, or delivery problems may strongly disparage the supplier.

If the potential source is a very small firm that has not previously exported, reference checks will be very difficult. A very small company's banking history may simply reflect a single account, Dun & Bradstreet will have no record of it, and its customers will all be other small firms in the same country. A plant survey will probably provide more and better information.

Location and Infrastructure

A few of these issues are in the supplier profile but a supplier's perception of the advantages of its location may differ greatly from a buyer's. A perfunctory evaluation of the supplier's location and the national infrastructure available to it are the least inexpensive tests before a plant survey.

A simple evaluation may be in shipping and insurance quotations from a freight forwarder for hypothetical shipments to and from the location. An "Ex Works" quotation will include all the costs of shipping, and documentation from the source's plant to the final destination. A "Delivered, Duty Paid" quotation will reflect the same costs for a shipment to the source. (Both these and other terms related to shipping and customs are presented in greater detail in Chapter 6.)

Such quotations are usually broken down to show the cost of each segment of transportation, plus any duties or fees that must be paid. They would therefore reflect local transportation costs and terminal or port fees in the source country, costs of obtaining export clearance or licenses if required, the cost of air or sea transport to and from the country, and import duties or customs and handling fees. When compared to similar quotations from other locations, large discrepancies in cost often reflect weak infrastructures. Asking for insurance quotes is a good measurement of shipping risk, either from political instability or poor transportation facilities.

Communications can be tested by merely timing the telephone calls and fax or telex inquiries to the potential source. Problems that occur in communicating during a supplier evaluation can be anticipated later. If it is nearly impossible to place or receive calls, or if fax and telex messages are answered only after long delays, the same will occur when sourcing through the supplier.

Plant Survey

Properly conducted, a plant survey should trace both the document and material flows of a customer order from placement to shipment. Every function should be examined to ensure that the supplier exercises the care and control appropriate to the product. Each operation should be governed by written procedures and every change in the procedures or the product should be fully and formally documented. For a suggested plant survey technique, see Figure 2.2.

A checklist or questionnaire is almost essential to avoid overlooking parts of the operation. The checklist can be mailed to the supplier well in advance of a visit, since it will take a considerable amount of time to fill out. Without adequate notice to the supplier, a survey may degenerate into little more than a perfunctory tour.

A plant survey is the final examination of supplier qualification. Intended to identify every deficiency of a supplier, a survey's scope and depth may be disquieting. Without the reasonable expectation of an order, many suppliers are reluctant to support one. Some will not accept a survey without a letter of intent to purchase or an order subject only to qualification and first article approval.

A thorough survey will include both the questionnaire and a visit to confirm the responses given. For the best understanding of a potential source's operations, review the questionnaire as part of a plant tour, observing each department while discussing it.

SUMMARY

The many business relationships of an experienced buyer provide the easiest way to locate an offshore supplier but many other ways exist. Foreign consulates are usually staffed to encourage trade. Many countries set up trade development boards in major U.S. cities. Foreign suppliers often exhibit at trade and industry shows in the United States. The buyer's bank, suppliers,

FIGURE 2–2
Plant Survey: Material, Document, and Information Flows

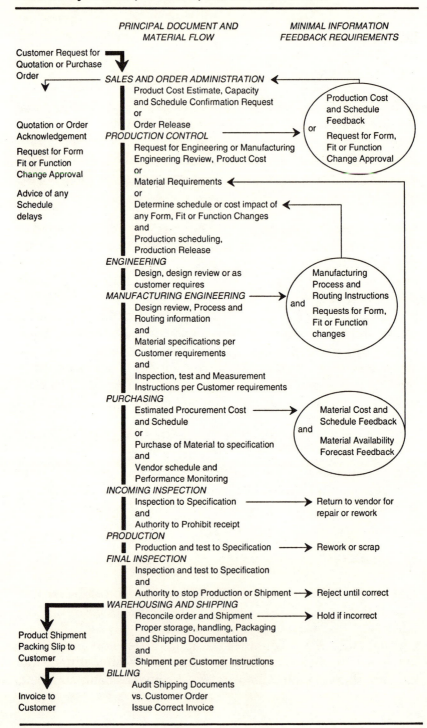

PRINCIPAL DOCUMENT AND MATERIAL FLOW

MINIMAL INFORMATION FEEDBACK REQUIREMENTS

Customer Request for Quotation or Purchase Order

SALES AND ORDER ADMINISTRATION
Product Cost Estimate, Capacity and Schedule Confirmation Request
or
Order Release

Production Cost and Schedule Feedback
or
Request for Form, Fit or Function Change Approval

Quotation or Order Acknowledgement

Request for Form Fit or Function Change Approval

Advice of any Schedule delays

PRODUCTION CONTROL
Request for Engineering or Manufacturing Engineering Review, Product Cost
or
Material Requirements
or
Determine schedule or cost impact of any Form, Fit or Function Changes
and
Production scheduling, Production Release

ENGINEERING
Design, design review or as customer requires

MANUFACTURING ENGINEERING
Design review, Process and Routing information
and
Material specifications per Customer requirements
and
Inspection, test and Measurement Instructions per Customer requirements

Manufacturing Process and Routing Instructions
and
Requests for Form, Fit or Function changes

PURCHASING
Estimated Procurement Cost and Schedule
or
Purchase of Material to specification
and
Vendor schedule and Performance Monitoring

Material Cost and Schedule Feedback
and
Material Availability Forecast Feedback

INCOMING INSPECTION
Inspection to Specification
and
Authority to Prohibit receipt

Return to vendor for repair or rework

PRODUCTION
Production and test to Specification

Rework or scrap

FINAL INSPECTION
Inspection and test to Specification
and
Authority to stop Production or Shipment

Reject until correct

WAREHOUSING AND SHIPPING
Reconcile order and Shipment
Proper storage, handling, Packaging and Shipping Documentation
and
Shipment per Customer Instructions

Hold if incorrect

Product Shipment Packing Slip to Customer

BILLING
Audit Shipping Documents vs. Customer Order
Issue Correct Invoice

Invoice to Customer

or customers may have overseas contacts. Some firms will locate a supplier for a fee or commission.

The cost and services of an intermediary in a purchase transaction vary widely and are readily negotiable. Several forms of international distribution channels are similar to those found in the United States but several other types exist as well. It is generally advantageous for a buyer to identify the primary manufacturer first, then negotiate for the services of an intermediary, if one is needed.

Independent small and midsize firms usually offer the best purchase opportunities to the U.S. buyer. Many primary sources may not wish to sell directly to a U.S. buyer or may be prevented from doing so. Foreign subsidiaries of U.S. companies, for example, may produce exclusively for their parent company. Many large multinationals sell only through distributors. Many companies, especially in Asia, are virtually held captive by their primary customer.

A rigorous survey and evaluation of prospective suppliers is a necessity when buying overseas. Many business practices and procedures may be lax, or simply different, offshore. Scrutiny of the supplier's communications, documents, and material flows may reveal deficiencies that could impair timely delivery of quality goods.

CHECKLIST

Ways of Locating a Potential Overseas Supplier
    Consulates and trade boards
    Personal acquaintances
    Suppliers and customers
    Export periodicals
    Trade shows
    Professional and industry associations
    Contract searches (a last resort)

Ignore Sources that Will Not Sell Direct

Large multinationals may sell only through distributors.

U.S. subsidiaries may have exclusive rights in United States.

Liaison offices facilitate primary sources' sales in United States but cannot sell.

Captive suppliers may be permitted to sell only through their major customer.

Considering the Use of an Intermediary

Does the size of the purchase warrant any extra effort the primary source may require? (Direct purchase costs less but requires more time and effort. Very small sources need to be closely monitored.)

Will the primary source need help in translation, or in obtaining documents or exporting?

Will source inspection be needed?

Is the intermediary authorized to act for the primary source?

Does the fee or commission warrant the added service the intermediary offers?

Who will bear the responsibility for the timely delivery? for rejected goods? for repair or rework?

Make the Initial Inquiry

Generate interest while avoiding commitment.

Express interest in the company; a continuing relationship is more interesting than a quick sale.

Present your company's profile: size, products, reputation.

Outline the product or service being sought—concise description, vague cost, and volume targets.

Don't exaggerate the business opportunity.

Request information that will help confirm the supplier's ability to perform.

Acknowledge how the supplier was identified, especially if through a personal introduction.

Focus on collecting information, not providing it.

Evaluate the Supplier

Begin with inquiries by mail, fax, or telephone, avoiding international travel expense.

Supplier Profile (Sample questionnaire in Appendix 2)
Reference and Credit Check
Location and Infrastructure
Plant Survey and Evaluation (Sample survey questionnaire
   in Appendix 2)

APPENDIX 2A: SAMPLE SUPPLIER PROFILE AND SURVEY QUESTIONNAIRES

SAMPLE SUPPLIER PROFILE QUESTIONNAIRE
Products
1. Is the company currently making a similar product?
2. Will the company's products compete with the proposed purchase?

FACILITIES AND EQUIPMENT
3. What is the size of the plant and approximate distribution among the various functions, particularly the production and warehouse areas?
4. What is the capacity and current utilization of the plant?
5. Is the facility owned or leased?
6. What utilities are available? Number of telephone lines? Public or private water? Available power, voltage and frequency? Is there any history of utility interruption?
7. What is the type, quantity, size, and age of equipment used?
8. What test and measurement equipment is used for incoming inspection and in-process measurement?
9. Does the equipment maintenance program include periodic calibration? Is the calibration program traceable to national or international standards?

ORGANIZATION AND PERSONNEL
10. How is the company organized? Are its executives members of the Board of Directors? What level (Vice President, Managing Director, Manager) are the executives of Manufacturing, Engineering, Sales, Finance?
11. Does the company do any original design or build, or assemble, only to specification? In what proportions?
12. Is a significant amount of work subcontracted? Do subcontractors supply any important subassemblies or processes? Is the plant dependent on any subcontractors for a difficult technology?
13. Is there a separate quality organization? Where does it report?

14. What are the total number of employees? Approximately how are they distributed among the major functions?

FINANCIAL
15. What is the ownership of the company? Is the majority of its stock held by its executives or board? Is its main bank a shareholders? Are any major customers also shareholders?
16. What is the company's annual sales revenue? Its capitalization? Debt-to-equity ratio? Please provide a recent income statement and balance sheet.

BANK AND CUSTOMER REFERENCES
"(Supplier) hereby grants permission to (buyer) to interview the customers named herein as references."

Name: _____ Phone (s) _____

Address: _____ Fax (s) _____

City: _____ State: _____ Zip: _____ Country: _____

Date established: _____ Parent Company: _____

Location of plant where work is to be performed: _____

Principal product or Services: _____ Percent of total: _____

Principal product or Services: _____ Percent of total: _____

Plant total area: (sq. ft.) _____ Production area: _____

Inspection area: _____ Indirect area: _____

Employees:	1st Shift	2nd Shift	3rd Shift	Total
Production				
Engineering				
Quality				
Admin/other				

Major Customers: _____ Percent of Capacity: _____

Major Customers: _____ Percent of Capacity: _____

Major Customers: _____ Percent of Capacity: _____

Sales contact: _____ Title: _____

Quality contact: _____ Title: _____

Finance contact: _____ Title: _____

1.0 ORDER ADMINISTRATION

1.1 Is there a formal routing for product costing?

1.2 Are Requests for Quotation handled by Order Administration?

1.3 Are Requests for Quotation routed through product costing?

1.4 Are acknowledgments returned to customers for all accepted orders?

1.5 Are all orders routed through Production Control or other organization responsible for plant scheduling before acceptance?

1.6 What is the customer return rate percent?

1.7 Are the latest customer drawings and specifications provided to manufacturing with an order?

2.0 ENGINEERING

2.1 Is there an in-house original design capability for this class of products?

2.2 Are engineering drawings maintained independent of production drawings?

2.3 Are engineering standards documented?

2.3 Is there a formal process to release engineering designs to manufacturing?

2.4 Is a formal design verification of prototypes held before manufacturing release?

2.5 Is a formal product verification of pre-production models held before production release?

2.6 Are Form, Fit, and Function reviews held for all product changes?

2.7 Does the part numbering system reflect Form, Fit, or Function changes?

2.8 Is there adequate expertise and experience to compensate for changes in personnel?

3.0 MANUFACTURING ENGINEERING

3.1 Is there a formal system for receiving and applying drawings, specifications, etc?

3.2 Do drawings and/or specifications indicate critical or functional characteristics?

3.3 Are Receiving Inspection and Manufacturing Test formally supplied with drawings, specifications, and critical or functional characteristics?

3.4 Are production drawings, process, or routing sheets traceable to customer drawings?

3.5 Is there adequate expertise and experience to compensate for changes in personnel?

4.0 PRODUCTION CONTROL

4.1 Is there a formal audit of drawings, specifications, bills-of-material, process, and routing sheets, etc. before release to Purchasing and Production?

4.2 Are lead time analyses performed for each Production Release? Manually? By computerized Material Requirements Planning?

4.3 Are production capacity analyses performed for each Production Release? Manually? By computerized Manufacturing Resource Planning?

4.4 is the majority of work performed by the vendor? If not, how much is subcontracted?

4.5 Is there a formal system for providing drawings, specifications, and critical or functional characteristics to Purchasing?

4.6 Are production drawings and specifications traceable to customer drawings?

4.7 Are all changes to product or process made subject to customer review and approval?

4.8 Is formal confirmation of production scheduling or release returned to Order Administration?

4.9 Is there a formal system for monitoring purchasing and production for an order?

4.10 Is there adequate expertise and experience to compensate for changes in personnel?

4.11 Does production control have the staff and resources to handle problems?

5.0 *PURCHASING*

5.1 Are purchasing lead times correctly reflected in production planning schedules?

5.2 Are drawings and specifications for purchased material formally transmitted to Purchasing?

5.3 Is purchasing documentation traceable to customer specifications?

5.4 Is purchase order documentation traceable to customer specifications?

5.5 Is there a vendor qualification program?

5.6 Is there an Approved Vendor List (AVL)?

5.6 Are samples of first articles required from vendors before acceptance of purchase?

5.7 Is there adequate expertise and experience to compensate for changes in personnel?

6.0 *PRODUCTION*

6.1 Is there a formal training program for production supervisors and workers when new products are introduced?

6.2 Are process and routing sheets with each Production Release?

6.3 Are process and routing sheets posted at each workstation or at each operation of production?

6.4 Is the quantity and size of equipment adequate to support orders?

6.5 Is the size of the physical plant adequate to support orders?

6.6 Are equipment and physical plant adequate to support increased volume?

6.7 Is production equipment properly maintained and stored?

6.8 Are tools properly stored and accounted for when not being used in production?

6.9 Is production equipment maintained through a systematic preventative maintenance program.

6.10 Is there a formal periodic equipment calibration program?

6.11 Is a Final Inspection or Audit documented and implemented?

6.12 Are adequate safeguards in place to prevent packing or shipment without Final Inspection?

7.0 QUALITY ASSURANCE

7.1 Are Quality and Reliability functions distinct from production?

7.2 Does the Quality have the authority to stop production or shipment?

7.3 Are inspection, test, and maintenance equipment calibrated on a regular preset schedule?

7.4 Are calibration frequencies adequate?

7.5 Are calibration standards traceable to national or international standards agencies?

7.6 Is there an adequate Incoming Inspection program?

7.7 Are adequate sample sizes in use?

7.8 Are samples of first articles from vendors adequately tested or inspected before acceptance?

7.9 Are Incoming Inspection records maintained by part and vendor?

7.10 Is there a continuous vendor surveillance program?

7.11 Are critical or major drawing or specifications checked pursuant to written inspection procedures?

7.12 Are any raw materials identified and traceable to certification reports?

7.13 Are tests of raw materials performed on regular, preset schedules?

7.14 Is there an adequate Corrective Action program for rejected purchases?

7.15 Could the vendor perform a Root Cause Analysis?

7.16 Is there adequate expertise and experience to compensate for changes in personnel?

8.0 WAREHOUSING

8.1 Are storage facilities adequate to prevent damage from overcrowding?

8.2 Are special facilities available to protect special materials?
8.3 Are storage locations marked?
8.4 Is the warehouse on a Perpetual Inventory or Cycle Count program?
8.5 Are storage locations subject to periodic audit?
8.6 Is discrepant material isolated from production material?
8.7 Are valuable materials under restricted access?

9.0 SHIPPING

9.1 Is the shipping facility adequate to prevent mixed shipments from overcrowding?
9.2 Are shipments verified against customer orders?
9.3 Is Final Inspection certification required for shipment?
9.4 Are controls adequate to ensure good packaging?
9.5 Are shipping procedures documented?

10.0 BILLING AND FINANCIAL

10.1 Do customer invoices require shipping verification?
10.2 Does accounting audit shipping and customer order information?
10.3 Are billing procedures documented?
10.4 Is the company publicly held?
10.5 Do its financial statements reflect adequate resources, reserves, and stability?
10.6 Are proposed purchases greater than 5 percent but less than 20 percent of annual sales?

11.0 FACILITY AND INFRASTRUCTURE

11.1 Is the physical plant safe and well maintained?
11.2 Are utilities adequate and reliable?
11.3 Is access to loading and unloading docks unrestricted?
11.4 Are transportation facilities (airport, harbor) within same-day access?
11.5 Are transportation facilities and capacity adequate?

11.6 Is international freight allowed unrestricted movement except by customs procedures?

11.7 Are communications facilities (telephone, telex, fax) adequate?

11.8 Can communication be kept confidential?

11.9 Are international communications unrestricted?

CHAPTER 3

CUSTOMS, CULTURE, AND CAUTION

We once spent the first three days of a visit to a potential Brazilian supplier getting to know each other. We visited for hours just making what can only be considered small talk. We were invited to meet his wife. We dined together, talked about politics, schools, and raising children. Those of us who had them showed him pictures of our wives and children, even our cars and boats.

One member of our group had to be reminded constantly to be patient, to bite his tongue a little longer. Normally the type who wanted to "get down to business" even at the office. He was unmarried as well, and couldn't even pass around any pictures. It was difficult to persuade him that this might be the normal way of doing business here.

Almost needless to say, when it was time to discuss business, things went very smoothly. We each knew what the other wanted and needed and quickly reached an agreement very acceptable to both of us. It bore little resemblance to the negotiations we had planned and imagined before arrival. The process was at least as successful as and far more comfortable than any lengthy bout at a conference table.

As much time will be used during the first visit to an offshore source getting acquainted as it will on discussing business. With few exceptions, business offshore depends on personal relations far more than in the United States. The business traveler should expect to be on the job, or on display, every waking hour when visiting an offshore supplier. Every aspect of the traveler's behavior will contribute to the impression made on prospective partners. An invitation for an evening out provides an opportunity for the hosts to observe a prospective customer at ease.

The traveler who can't differentiate between "firm" and "obnoxious" shouldn't represent a company offshore; no amount of preparation will compensate for a lack of manners.

While the process of developing relationships in South America is probably the most lengthy and personal that will be encountered, the business traveler will be on display in a number of situations not ostensibly related to business. Whether in an initial introductory meeting with the source, dining out, during an evening on the town, or playing golf, the impression created by the traveler will be the one brought to the negotiating table.

AMERICAN IMAGE OFFSHORE

Friendly, warm, likable, vibrant, motivated, goal oriented, successful—these are all attributes Americans admire in others and try to achieve for themselves. Overseas, these qualities are as likely to be viewed as shortcomings as assets.

The friendly American who introduces her- or himself has probably overstepped the limits of propriety everywhere but in another English-speaking country. Elsewhere, such behavior is forward, brash, rude, or arrogant, depending on local notions of privacy, attitudes toward strangers, and other cultural factors. The reaction to a woman who does so will be more severe; in most countries it is expected only of a prostitute. A warm hug, or slap on the back, is even less welcome. Even the abraco (traditional male embrace) of South America is limited to those whose relationship has reached a stage that permits it. To a Japanese or Chinese, who still greet each other with a bow, and only recently adopted the handshake for dealing with Westerners, such behavior is offensive.

Humility is a grace little practiced in the United States but much respected in the rest of the world. Abroad, Americans are generally perceived as self-aggrandizing. They are certainly seen as being more willing to speak than listen, even when the topic is not themselves. The habit of finishing someone else's sentence is not seen as proof of a quick intelligence, but as impatient, intolerant, and rude.

The American who wants to forego the pleasantries and get

down to business is apt to be regarded as aggressive, even ruth-less. To many cultures, work is not good, only a necessity for survival. Many foreign businesspeople may resent the intrusion of business after working hours and will be offended at having to spend their leisure time entertaining a guest who doesn't have the courtesy to relax with them.

Yet from country to country many American traits are ad-mired and behavior that is inappropriate in one country may be perfectly acceptable in another. The Japanese will be interested in whether the customer is married and how many children are in the family, but businesspeople in Hong Kong would consider such a conversation "inefficient." The bluntness of an Eastern European would be offensive anywhere in Asia. The openness of the Australians may not be a surprise, but the reserve of New Zealand may come as a shock.

Some business etiquette and protocol will help the sourcing traveler to cope with the array of accepted behaviors when mov-ing around the world, but observation is probably the best tool. Whenever in doubt, let the host take the lead and follow the example.

WOMEN TRAVELING ON BUSINESS

I had been in Korea several days with a couple of other people from my company. After a long, but successful, negotiation, we had dinner with the supplier at a traditional restaurant where you sit on the floor. I had worn a suit to look as professional as possible and had to drop to the floor because the skirt was so tight.

After dinner they took us back to the hotel and told me to go to my room. They were going to take the men to a Keiseng House. But doing business overseas is no worse than it is here.

Possibly the most telling part of this manager's comments is that it is "no worse" offshore than in the United States. Almost universally, the complaint of women sourcing offshore is that conversation is invariably directed at the men present, not to the woman, even if she is the senior member of the visiting party. Most indicate that they are treated with equal or greater courtesy when overseas but suffer far more from the perception that women will have little to contribute to a negotiation.

Being left at the hotel while the men visit a Keiseng House, the Korean equivalent of a Geisha House, is the exception rather than the rule. Although women in business are more of an anomaly in Asia than elsewhere, the courtesy extended to business visitors anywhere will usually ensure that all will be treated equally. Normally, the evening described above would have ended after dinner, with nobody going to the Keiseng House.

The decision to wear a suit to appear as professional as possible was a correct one; only hindsight would suggest deep pleats. Conservative business dress is always appropriate for meetings and some conservatism advisable even for leisure hours. The manager who made the comments above suggests that slacks be avoided. Although they are worn by women almost everywhere they may not be regarded as appropriate for business. She notes that they are especially awkward where the facilities are primitive.

Although the professional woman can do little to change the attitudes she will encounter when sourcing offshore, she can do a few things to help avoid being patronized, especially if she is the senior visitor. First, she should utilize the precedence messages implicit in the order of business card exchange and seating, both of which are more fully discussed below. Business cards, as well, can support the message; if they are of better stock, oiled, or the only ones that have the local language translation on the reverse, the distinction will be evident. Next, even if she is not senior, she should answer any questions that should have been directed to her. Although doing this without interrupting may require the tacit agreement of anyone traveling with her, the supplier will eventually recognize which are her areas of expertise or responsibility and react accordingly.

INTRODUCTORY MEETINGS

The first face-to-face meeting with an offshore supplier is usually a brief and courteous introduction of the principal players in the negotiations. The introductions are of both the companies and the individuals who will be involved in the transaction. Two things are thus established: the relative positions of the individuals and the identity of the one who will make the major decisions during the negotiations, whether present at the meeting or not.

Most such meetings may not, and probably won't, go into great personal detail except in South America. Nevertheless, business topics normally intrude into the meeting only to the extent needed to acquaint the supplier with the visitor's company. An annual report, company profile, or data sheets should have been forwarded with the initial inquiry. Additional copies should be brought to the introductory meeting along with pictures of the factory or office and anything else that may help the supplier develop a personal picture of the company.

Visitors should also be prepared to explain their company's organization and their position in it. They should know which countries their company does business in. If the company has a direct presence in the host's country, members of that organization should be at the introductory meeting. If they aren't at the meeting, some explanation of their absence is appropriate.

If the prospective supplier is a large firm, and the visitor has not been corresponding with the executive level of the firm, an executive may attend this get-acquainted session. This executive will acknowledge the discussions but won't mention any detailed knowledge of them. The presence at the meeting is specifically to introduce the two companies to each other. There is another clear message here: The executive will not participate in the negotiations but will have the final say. The buyer will continue to negotiate with whomever has been communicating, but the executive's approval will be needed. Even though the meeting has identified a decision maker, no attempt should be made at negotiation. The executive expects someone of lower rank to negotiate in all aspects except final approval authority and the possibility of disapproving.

Business Cards

Business cards are a more important element of commerce abroad than in the United States, particularly in Asia. Some articles discussing business card etiquette seem to go overboard in describing the complexity of the card ritual and subsequent notation, filing, and management of them. Nevertheless, understanding how some cultures use them may be helpful in putting them in perspective.

A little background in understanding why they are so important in some places might be helpful. At least four factors are significant: (1) the relative importance attributed to rank and position; (2) poor telephone directory services; (3) difficult addressing systems; and (4) differences among written and spoken languages.

Despite the egalitarian sheen that has appeared worldwide, rank and position still play a greater role outside the United States. The business card of the number two man in the number two section says so: "Deputy Section manager, Section 2, such-and-such organization." The American business card that reads "Sales Engineer" is apt to result in several questions aimed at trying to more precisely define the position in the company. If the position can be better defined than it is on the card, such information should be offered when it is presented. If two or three visitors have the same title, each in a different division, the distinction should be noted. When questions or problems arise it is very helpful to know where to go for answers. This need applies both to buyer and seller.

Telephone directories in most underdeveloped or newly developed countries are poor to nonexistent. This is especially true for those which also have to contend with a Chinese character language or multiple nationalities and languages, as in Russia. Even the operators' resources are limited when pronunciation alone is insufficient to identify a person. English language commercial publications, found in many of the better hotels, are generally incomplete as they include only the advertisers or subscribers who have paid for their inclusion. A business card file is often the only directory.

A long history of uncontrolled growth has resulted in the development of utter mazes in many of the older cities of the world. Mushrooming American suburbs have created situations that can be just as confusing. California's Silicon Valley can be as difficult as Paris; the same street may have as many names as the little municipalities through which it passes, changing each time it crosses from San Jose into Santa Clara into Mountain View. The traveler will need the supplier's business card for the taxi driver almost everywhere. The supplier will have as great a need for the buyer's card.

The very old Chinese ideographs are widely used throughout Asia and are common to many very different languages. In each language the same symbol has the same meaning but may be pronounced entirely differently. As the various nations around China recognized the need for a written language, they adopted the Chinese characters and forced them to fit their own spoken language. Some countries adopted both the Chinese characters and language while maintaining their own spoken language in parallel. As a result, knowing how to pronounce a person's name may not provide any clue as to how to write it. Many names are as common as Smith, Jones, and Brown: Patel in India, Watanabe in Japan, Chan in China and Taiwan. Everywhere, business cards help avoid the embarrassment of misaddressing the local equivalent of Bob Jones when talking to Sam Jones.

A final word: Bring plenty. Everyone met will expect to receive one. Not offering one implies that the person is not important enough to get one. That person might become the most important contact in the supplier's company and will have been insulted in the first meeting. Make copies if the supply is exhausted; cut them out and apologize for the problem.

Introductions and Card Exchange

Exchanging business cards is one of the protocols for establishing seniority and precedence. Even when the introductions are very informal and business cards are casually flipped across the table, the senior members of the two companies will initiate the process and, having done so, will have identified themselves as such. In Asia, where all the reasons for using business cards exist, the exchange is more elaborate but clearly illustrates how precedence can be demonstrated: The respective parties file past the other in descending order of importance of the company's members and each person exchanges cards with every member of the party. Naturally, by the time the most junior are greeting each other, everyone else is already seated.

If driving a stick shift is the most demanding coordination required of modern man, the actual act of exchanging business cards in Asia must be a close second, especially if the host insists on bowing according to custom and then tosses in a Western handshake to demonstrate a worldly attitude. The complexity of the exchange may leave the uninitiated feeling graceless and uncoordinated. The process is simple. Offer a business card with both hands, grasping it between the thumb and forefinger of each. Bow and say "My name is . . . "

Straighten up and swap cards, offering with the right and receiving with the left. Shake hands and say "I'm pleased to meet you." In a conference room full of people, keep as many cards as needed in the left hand. Keep track of who is who. Lay the cards on the table, arranged the same way their owners are seated.

There are a few more complex variations of the exchange. Japanese men bow with their hands at their sides from a slight, respectful distance and then step forward with their cards. They both offer and receive the card with both hands, a custom that applies to both business cards and gifts. In this case the exchange is a one-two, not a swap. The abbreviated ritual above, however, will let most Americans effect the exchange with at least a little grace. Generally, only the Japanese retain the custom of offering the card the same way as a gift, but the custom may be encountered elsewhere. A bow isn't needed in countries where the handshake is the common gesture.

Seating

As anyone who has seen pictures of a summit conference has noticed, seating arrangements are a clear indication of seniority. In business meetings between companies, the senior visitor sits with back to the window at the center table, or, if there is no window, then opposite the door. Number two sits on number one's right and number three on the left. The same will happen on the other side of the table. This arrangement is in strong contrast with boardroom seating and other meetings within a single organization where a single individual dominates and sits at the head of the table. If the room has armchairs and a sofa, the sofa is the visitor's and will usually be placed with its back to a window or opposite the door.

Upon entering the room, the senior visitor can stake out this position with a notebook or papers and remain standing to be introduced to the senior member of the host team. After being introduced, the visitor will remain in the same place as the other members of the host party file up to introduce themselves.

ENTERTAINMENT

Business entertainment is expense account entertainment. Visitors, therefore, are generally entertained in places their hosts don't frequent except when entertaining and can't afford except on an expense account. Compared to most industrialized or newly developed countries, the United States is particularly stingy when it comes to allowing entertainment deductions. Outside the United States, except for the Peoples' Republic of China, almost the opposite is true. European, Latin American, and Asian countries are either more liberal with their expense deductions or have more deeply ingrained habits of evasion. In Asia, Japan in particular has very liberal entertainment allowances, generally several percent of a contract's value, plus personal allowances for executives that are often comparable to their salaries.

Given the often exorbitant expense of the entertainment catering to this market and the expense account largesse available to fund it, business entertaining offers foreign businesspeople the chance to enjoy what they otherwise can't. This bonus is normally distributed by rank, the more senior members of a supplier's team eating and drinking out more frequently, or more expensively. Frequently, the group of people entertaining a customer dwindles markedly after dinner. Some of the more junior members of the group slip off and go home, their share limited to dinner.

Entertainment like this can lead to an exhausting regimen and one that many have suspected to be partly negotiating tactics. One or two members of the host's staff will entertain a customer after the first day's meeting, others the second evening, and still others the third. A buyer infrequently will be negotiating with the previous evening's drinking partners but more often with those who will next be entertaining. The process can be debilitating. It is not impolite to plead exhaustion from jet lag to the junior "teams" and suggest they continue the evening, if they wish, by themselves. Everyone will seem happy with this arrangement.

The places in which business visitors are first entertained normally differ markedly from local habits, especially in cost and venue. They are much more apt to be large, or at least expensive, clubs, often with floor shows. They will probably not be the comfortable "watering hole" the host usually drops in on the way home, at least not until the buyer and supplier have become well acquainted. In fact, unless very certain of the circumstances, a business traveler shouldn't "go back to that nice place of last night" alone. It may have been a private club and some embarrassment may result for the visitor, for the club's management, and, when he learns of the attempt, for the host. It will almost certainly have been expensive.

Dining

Dining is an extended opportunity to develop personal relationships. Although certainly a part of doing business, business discussions are normally no part of the dinner conversation. The expectations of a business traveler in good restaurants all over the world will be the same. Whether a French restaurant in Paris or Buenos Aires, the dinner and service will vary only with the skill of the staff. This section therefore focuses only on the few times real differences in the dining experience may be encountered—the relatively formal private dinners to which the traveler may be invited in South America and sometimes Europe, and the unique experiences that may be encountered in Asia.

Genteel good manners and pleasure in formality heavily influence South American gatherings. Much of the protocol normally reserved for very formal dinners in the United States may be observed in even small dinner parties in South America. Handwritten invitations may be sent for larger dinners. The recipient should have the good manners to respond. The absence of an "RSVP" (an acronym Americans have borrowed from the French) on the invitation is not an excuse for not doing so.

Dinner will be preceded by a gathering for introductions, an exchange of pleasantries, perhaps an aperitif and very often beer. The visitor, presumably the stranger to the group, may be presented to the guests individually by the host. The whole affair may superficially resemble an American cocktail party but it certainly isn't. Guests will normally enter the room with a bow and politely greet all the other guests quietly and with a handshake. The visitor will be expected to do the same, except that introductions will be added to the process. In very traditional families, men and women may separate themselves in the room but this practice is becoming increasingly rare.

Very special occasions, such as the signing of a major agreement or formation of a company, may be celebrated by a banquet. Faced for the first time with the full complement of utensils that can accompany such a meal, one need only remember to start with those at the outside of either side of the plate and work in, then with those at the top of the plate and work up.

These formalities may sound rigid, but in practice they are not. The South Americans accomplish this with an easy grace. It is not difficult to imagine that they see themselves as the last practicing bastion of chivalry.

A popular misconception equates Japanese food with the truly exotic. In fact, the traveler will probably encounter a wider variety of unusual offerings in Taiwan, where virtually all the Chinese provinces are represented, than anywhere else. In all likelihood dinner in Japan will be one of several dishes normally considered holiday fare: Sukiyaki is a delicious way of eating beef, as is mizutake or "shabu-shabu." Barbequed eel is delicious and most Americans try to duplicate the barbequed chicken, "yaki-tori," when they get home. A few dishes may be dismaying. In a country where fish is often eaten raw, providing signs of freshness is a matter of courtesy. American lobster restaurants, which let the diner choose, do the same thing. A common way to demonstrate the freshness of shashimi, slices of raw fish, is to fillet the fish live leaving the head and tail connected by the backbone. The raw fish is served on a bed of greens laid over the backbone with the head and tail of the fish exposed. During the meal the fish gapes or the tail quivers, proving its freshness.

The better Japanese restaurants provide private dining rooms. They invariably are floored with "tatami," grass mats. Guests sit on pillows on the tatami at a low table. In a few restaurants a pit underneath the table permits sitting at the table as if on a chair. Shoes are removed before walking on tatami; a Japanese expression for a rude and boorish person is one who doesn't remove his or her shoes. Men should pack a pair of loafers when visiting Japan to avoid having to tie and untie their shoes. Because Americans need to move around a little when sitting on the floor, it is recommended that women pack a few of their fuller skirts when visiting anywhere in Asia.

Seating in a private room resembles that of the conference room; again the senior guest's place is at the middle of the table, generally opposite the door. Many private dining rooms will have a picture alcove with a scroll or flower arrangement, or both. A highly polished natural post forms one side of the alcove. The guest seat is in front of the post, with back to it. The host will sit opposite the guest. Unlike the conference room seating, however, members of two companies comingle. The visitors' number two person should take a seat next to the senior person in the supplier's company. The supplier's number two will sit next to the senior guest. No matter what the rank, if it is necessary to include a translator, that person will probably sit beside the senior guest.

The round table common to a Chinese meal shouldn't be much more difficult. The senior guest still sits farthest from the door. The visiting counterpart will be seated nearly opposite, an even number of seats away so the two teams can alternate. At very large tables the diminution of rank appears to resemble a star. A visitor shouldn't try to organize such a group; the hosts will point out the principal seats and let everyone else find their own.

Don't underestimate the number of courses in the Chinese meal. Ten or twelve are common at a banquet and six or eight are common at an informal gathering. Take only a bit of the many dishes that will appear. If some of the offerings are too exotic, they can be unobtrusively avoided. Plenty more will fill the table. Near the end of almost every meal a baked or steamed fish will arrive. The senior visitor is honored with the head, and especially the eyes. Considered a delicacy, the host will probably be grateful if they are passed up.

Breakfast is the meal at which international travelers have the most difficulty accommodating foreign food. This applies equally to the American abroad and to a foreign guest in the United States. Imagine sitting down to a breakfast of cold raw egg and plain rice with dried seaweed, or cold dried fish with bean curd soup and seaweed, or sour milk on cereal with cold cuts. To someone accustomed to this fare, a pair of eggs fried in butter, greasy fried potatoes, heavy bread lathered with butter or margarine, and strips of bacon is an equally miserable way to start the day.

Almost everyone will agree that one's own breakfast is the hardest meal to replace. The typical American probably won't enjoy a Japanese breakfast or the cold cereal with sour milk in Sweden. Unless schedule pressure leaves no other option, avoid breakfast meetings. Even then, arrange to have them in a hotel restaurant that caters to both the foreign and western diets.

Nightlife

Local nightlife and drinking habits differ somewhat in different countries and regions. Travelers in Europe will find habits similar to those in the United States with only a few exceptions. First, cocktail parties are an American phenomenon and are unlikely to be encountered in Europe or anywhere else. Next, drinking may be confined to dinner. In Europe, after dinner drinking may be a significant extension of the meal, good conversation the entertainment. Americans starting an evening with a cocktail or two, anticipating a break for a change of venue after dinner, will be at a distinct disadvantage if wine continues to flow through dessert and coffee. If one sherry appears to be the normal aperitif, follow the host's lead.

The same warning will apply in South America, although the drinks may be different. With the exception of Chile, few countries in South America have succeeded in making good wines, and certainly not enough for the drink to be widely popular. Otherwise, the Latin American countries take their drinking cues from Europe. After dinner drinking at the table is common, but the excellent beer may take the place of wine. Also popular are several sugar cane based liquors. A variety of drinks are based on rum and a couple of potent local products. Beware of before dinner cocktails, beer during dinner, and then something exotic later.

Nightlife in South America will resemble neither the European cabarets nor the hostess bars of Asia. The nearest parallels are Las Vegas shows with the added twist of some audience participation. The costumes are lavish but scanty. The staging is elaborate, often involving the large, hydraulically raised stages reminiscent of the U.S. spectaculars of the 30s. Customers often participate in the show.

Asian nightlife differs markedly from the rest of the world both in drinking habits and the almost exclusively male orientation. "Hostesses" are found in nearly every bar and club to sit and converse with their predominantly male customers, to feed the ego, prolong the stay, and sell more drinks. Women are not unwelcome; many affluent young couples frequent the clubs, especially those with floor shows, but Western women may be uncomfortable. In addition to the sexual innuendo, which is common, merely watching her male companions being fawned over may be embarrassing. Nevertheless, since the hostess is being paid 20 to 30 dollars an hour to be entertaining, even female customers are catered to as assiduously as possible.

There is a common misconception that all bar hostesses are prostitutes. Although many are, they are equally likely not to be. The prettier, and therefore better paid, hostesses can earn upwards of $50,000 a year. Many moonlight as hostesses, working days in normal jobs elsewhere. Although prostitution is common in Taiwan and rampant in Bangkok, and though Singapore's "Dirty Clubs" and many clubs in Hong Kong cater to clients looking for sex, the hostess in a typical establishment might just as easily be a college girl working evenings.

Hostess club protocol is pretty much the same everywhere. The party will be seated by an usher or floor manager at a table, booth, or private room. The private rooms, common in Taiwan, are generally glass-fronted and are more to make conversation possible over the blare of a disco band than for privacy. Each person leaves room for a hostess, several of which will file in shortly after the guests are seated. The hostess assigned to a visitor will have been chosen for her ability to speak English, even if she can't manage it very well. If she can't, the visitor will probably spend the evening playing rather silly drinking games. If she can, and especially if she's a working student, entertaining conversation is possible. A hostess will be assigned as a courtesy, even if the visitor is a woman traveling alone, to give everyone an equal chance at conversation but the situation is improbable.

Golf

Given the worldwide rage for golf, and its frequent use as an extension of the meeting room, a business etiquette has risen around it. With enough time and the relationships built on a couple of visits, a business visitor who has indicated any interest in the game will undoubtedly be invited to play. Normally, a player with a club membership will pay all the expenses of a guest, and the guest reciprocates when acting as host.

Several factors require a modification of this etiquette among international travelers. First, reciprocity can't be guaranteed. Very few businesspeople can schedule business travel with much certainty. Short notice, the schedules of business counterparts, flight availability, and a horde of other factors leave few opportunities for the game at all.

Next, avid golfers will try to play as many different courses as possible, particularly famous ones. Neither buyer nor seller is likely to be a member of one of the famous courses. Therefore, when playing one, each will pay their own greens fees and no obligation to reciprocate is incurred. If the buyer's U.S. facility is within a few hours of a famous course, Pebble Beach for example, suggest that when an opportunity to reciprocate arises, the game will be played there. Very likely, the opportunity to play one of these courses will be appreciated no matter how poor a golfer the host may be. The host will often respond by getting a starting time on a spectacular course in the home country the next time, or even as a result of the suggestion.

TOUCHY SUBJECTS

Social interaction outside the meeting room will include discussion of a wide range of topics not encountered in negotiation, with the increased risk of unknowingly saying something that the supplier may find offensive or embarrassing. Although it should be obvious that the obscene or vulgar have no place in these discussions, the frankness with which Americans are accustomed to address everything is frequently discomforting to others outside the United States.

The best advice on how to handle touchy subjects is to avoid them. This advice doesn't apply to difficult business situations, of course, which must be addressed. But it won't help business to point out the brutalities of the police to the Koreans or to disparage socialism to the Swedish.

A lively political debate after work may be a refreshing change after a day negotiating, but don't initiate one. The hosts should lay the ground rules. Even then, approach the conversation with caution. Unless it's impossible to do so, use U.S. or third country examples to support an argument while letting the host provide local perspectives.

Don't be surprised if some uncomfortable issues arise: More people outside the U.S. are aware of corruption, poverty, homelessness, violence, and medical care problems in the United States than the reverse. On the other hand, don't miss these opportunities either. The professional who displays some knowledge of events outside the narrow scope of business can only benefit at the negotiating table from whatever degree of respect the knowledge earns. It doesn't hurt to admit that the United States has some problems. It will help to know what is being done about them, and discuss with others what might be done.

Language and Humor

Some of the funniest things Americans encounter overseas are misuse of English in both its written and spoken forms. Can the joke be shared without insulting the perpetrator? Probably not, so save it for home.

Someone once observed that England and the United States

are two countries separated by a common language. An American businessman received a platter of chicken in his lap when he said he was "stuffed." The apologetic hostess, an Australian, had been so surprised to hear he was pregnant ("stuffed" in local slang) that she lost control of the tray. He was almost equally disconcerted when she invited him to "knock her up" the following morning, until he discovered she meant awaken her with a knock on the door. These anecdotes are probably apocryphal but imagine the misunderstandings possible with non-native speakers.

Humor, or what passes for it in each culture, is probably the last part to cross the language barrier, or culture barrier. Grammatically correct language is first, then idiom, then slang, each of which are successively more ephemeral. Humor relies heavily on the startling or surprising juxtaposition of two elements of the same culture. For example, one of the few jokes that can survive cross-cultural translation involves a pilot who told his doctor that he hadn't had sex since 1958. When the doctor expresses surprise, the pilot says "but it's only 2130." The joke succeeds only because all of its elements are common to many cultures; the common year numbering system and the use of military time by airlines. An almost complete knowledge of a culture is needed to know what juxtapositions will be surprising.

Be careful to the point of avoiding attempts at humor. This admonition applies especially to observations about the host's culture that are humorous when juxtaposed with U.S. norms. No one likes to be the brunt of a joke, especially if it arises from their own ignorance. Save funny observations for those who will appreciate them.

GIFTS

In many parts of the world the exchange of gifts is part of the process of establishing a business relationship, but the pattern varies from nonexistent to a prolonged ritual depending on where the business is being conducted. The relative emphasis on form versus substance will vary as greatly. Since gift exchange patterns vary somewhat all over the world, there is not a comprehensive etiquette. In practice, following the supplier's lead is generally safe.

Gifts should generally fit the following guidelines:

1. They should not be given in expectation of anything, but for past performance or cooperation.

2. They would reasonably be given to anyone else in the same position.

3. They should not be personal.

4. They should definitely not be extravagant.

There are certainly exceptions to these guidelines. The Communist Chinese frown on gifts of any sort, despite rampant internal graft. A very inexpensive observation of someone's hobby or circumstances is all that may be acceptable—perhaps a stamp for a collector, a theme T-shirt for their child, or a small jar of coffee as a special change from tea.

In these exchanges the significance of the gift is in its appropriateness to the person and situation, not in its value. The de-emphasis of value, in fact, may be important. The point the gift is intended to convey is that a personal relationship may develop, that some understanding of the individual outside the business context has evolved, and that some rapport has been established.

The normal exchange of Christmas trinkets among Western businesspeople is only one pattern of business gift giving. Long rituals of gift exchange may be encountered in the Far East. Here form dominates. The gifts themselves seem to have little relationship to either the business at hand or the individuals involved. Many will appear to be valueless trinkets, although they may actually be very expensive. A clearly methodical escalation of the value of the gifts and the status of the people in the organization giving and receiving them will become evident. After a long association, it is often difficult to remember what was received from whom, and what was given in exchange. Notes on business cards are a good vehicle for keeping track.

In Latin America, flowers are frequently sent in appreciation of a courtesy. Flowers should also be brought to dinner at a private home; they may be sent before larger functions. Sending thank-you notes is equally common. Sincere thanks are reflected in a handwritten note, not in a typed one. Both courtesies are observed in Europe but not to the extent that they are in Latin America.

Giving nothing at all at a first meeting is quite appropriate. The supplier may present a mechanical pencil with the company's logo or some other item equally appropriate for a trade fair giveaway. Reciprocation should only be done in kind, that is, with another corporate logo. Both seller and buyer will have begun getting their name known in the other firm.

The first gift will normally be offered only when it is clear that some process has begun. The seller is the first to give something, usually a trinket of little intrinsic value. Quite often these are local handcrafted items or other mementos of the sort found at curio stands in the country. The seller is not only starting the ritual but also supporting the local economy while doing so.

The gift will probably be presented by the senior member of the supplier's company, normally somebody who has attended previous meetings. It will be offered to the senior visitor. In essence, the gift implies, "We recognize something has started and are willing to invest fifty cents to keep it going."

Always attempt to reciprocate in kind. Give much the same sort of trinket as was received. Let the supplier escalate the exchange, including either expanding the number of people involved in the exchange or the value of the gifts. Recognize rank with only subtle differences in the items. The initial gift will probably have been presented at the end of the first meeting. Reciprocate before the serious discussions of the next meeting begin, without fanfare.

Staying within the American culture in selecting gifts, rather than trying to understand and emulate the host's culture has several advantages. It will help avoid the possibly expensive situation of a quid pro quo exchange where the host is defining the exchange. Furthermore, choosing gifts will be easier. Choose something that reflects the American country and culture, something that demonstrates this heritage to the supplier. If and when the exchanges begin to escalate, it will still be possible to keep pace inexpensively. A coffee table book of local scenery or attractions, California or New York wines, maple syrup, Southwest Indian jewelry, Appalachian handcrafts, and so on are all suitable and available in prices ranging from the ridiculous to the sublime.

In Japan, in mainland China, and in some other parts of Asia, gifts are not opened in front of the giver. If the receiver does not appreciate the gift, the giver will be ashamed of having selected it. Offer thanks for it and put it away for later.

Shopping

This is one of the few activities where a traveler may be alone, if there is time. When looking for something in particular, however, it may be worthwhile to mention it to the host. Suppliers will probably be more than happy to direct, or even take, their visitors to someplace they know.

Bargaining, dickering, or haggling is more commonplace abroad, especially in Asia and South America. Knowing where bargaining is possible is almost as important as knowing how, the latter really depending on an ability to express real or feigned reluctance to a price. In Europe, for the most part, the better stores in the better districts have firm prices. Opportunities to dicker will generally occur only with street vendors. In China, on the other hand, haggling will occur almost everywhere except for a few department stores and a few shops that literally have a sign saying (in Chinese) "No bargaining."

Discounts are generally forthcoming, if requested, in the Far East. Haggling over price is expected in the Middle East and in much of South America, except in the finer stores. Note the distinction between asking for a discount in the Far East and haggling. Perhaps it's a distinction without a difference but, in the countries noted for politeness, a courteous refusal generally meets with more success than an argument. On the other hand Greek and Turkish vendors seem disappointed if they can't yell a little.

If in doubt about whether a given place will dicker a little, a good approach to starting a negotiation if one is unaccustomed to bargaining, is to say something like "I'd only planned to spend . . . " or "I only budgeted so much for . . . " Even places that don't normally expect to negotiate their prices may respond.

SUMMARY

Although customs vary widely, modest good manners should be all a buyer needs to work with offshore sources. Cementing personal relationships should be the goal of early meetings.

The aggressive, goal oriented, successful American may not be appreciated for these virtues. Overseas, these characteristics are as likely to be viewed as shortcomings as assets.

First meetings are generally for introductions, not negotiations. They provide an opportunity to learn who the players are and to identify the decision makers.

The business traveler is on display all the time when visiting a potential source, not only in the meeting room. Whether dining, on the town, or playing golf care should be exercised to present the best image possible.

CHECKLIST

1. Carry plenty of business cards. If time permits, have them printed with translations on the back, especially for trips to Asia.
2. Take annual reports, other introductory corporate literature, enough for each company to be visited, plus spares.
3. Small gifts, if it is time to reciprocate. Company-logo trinkets such as pens or day timers are appropriate on a first visit.
4. Clothing appropriate to both business and after-work situations that may be encountered. Remember that tropical heat and humidity may make extra changes desirable.
5. Enough time in the schedule to get acquainted.

CHAPTER 4

NEGOTIATING OUTSIDE YOUR OWN CULTURE

In the early 1970s an American marketing executive was negotiating the sale of a product line to Hitachi. The products were not well suited for the market so the executive spent much of the time promoting himself. Known for loudly proclaiming a very high opinion of himself, he told Mr. Misu, then Hitachi's vice president of marketing, that all the program would need was adequate marketing skills, which he, the executive, would be pleased to provide.

Several fruitless days later, over coffee in Mr. Misu's office, the executive was referred to an article in *Newsweek*, "The New Marketing Masters," which reviewed the dramatic success of Japanese marketing in the United States. Most of the first page of the article was a picture of Mr. Misu, seated at the same desk with the coffee.

The executive had prepared so poorly for the discussions that he hadn't bothered to learn with whom he would be negotiating. In addition, both his self-aggrandizement and disparaging comments were insulting to the Japanese. The negotiations had probably failed during their first few minutes.

There are plenty of books on negotiating. This isn't one of them. As its title indicates, this chapter is about negotiating in situations where the people on opposite sides of the table bring little in common to the discussions.

The chapter examines a few of the points a primer on negotiating might cover, but does not attempt to offer any new negotiating techniques. Instead, it reviews basic rules of negotiating in the context of doing business offshore. The reason for this review is to accent the importance of the basics in long-distance and cross-cultural negotiations, not to offer instruction in negotiating. And, though addressing the basics, it concentrates on presenting them within issues more or less unique to intercultural negotiation.

Primary among the important basics is the need for clear objectives and, certainly, for adequate preparation and planning. In addition to the cultural issues of the previous chapter, logistic and communications problems can severely impede negotiating offshore. The costs of international travel often preclude more than one meeting and many negotiations therefore become a single marathon session. Without clear objectives, a thorough definition of the product requirements, and explicit cost or other performance targets, backed up, with an understanding of what is reasonably possible, few such negotiations will be completely successful.

Written preparation, usually ignored domestically, is highly advisable for negotiations held outside the United States. The effort and inconvenience of travel, the excitement and confusion of other cultures, and the very real impact of jet lag are tiring at a minimum, and unavoidably detrimental to anyone's concentration. Added to these are the myriad new requirements of doing business offshore, the many issues of language, currency, importing, and so on, which greatly complicate negotiations. Written backup will be an invaluable reminder of issues that would otherwise be overlooked or neglected, often to the detriment of whoever forgot them.

Perhaps the best reason for good preparations for negotiating offshore is that the overseas suppliers are usually better prepared than their U.S. counterparts. U.S. business has recognized only recently the importance of industrial intelligence to the Japanese, this despite the fact that for many years their research departments openly, and legally, collected and analysed massive amounts of data in the United States. Small companies in other countries may not be as well prepared for a negotiation as the Japanese but may have access to national services established to promote trade. They will often have researched both the potential buyer and the general conditions of trade in the U.S. industry.

To avoid any confusion in the use of them, following is a brief preview of the words *objective, strategy, tactics,* and *options.*

Although the notion of a *war out there* may have been belabored enough already, the terms are probably still the best applicable ones. An *objective* is what is sought, whether lower prices, greater reliability, or a more responsive supplier. A *strategy* is the means to achieve an objective—shop around for the best pricing, impose stricter quality controls, or replace a current supplier. *Tactics* are how to keep the negotiation centered on the strategic path. Penetrating the supplier's cost structure, listening for weaknesses and strengths, and generating competition are all good tactical moves. *Options* are alternatives. A buyer needs to know whether something other, or less, than the original request can be accepted and still achieve the objective.

SETTING OBJECTIVES

1. Product specifications, price, quantity, quality, and delivery targets;
2. A range of expectations: optimistic, target, and unacceptable;
3. Acceptable trade-offs.

Product Specifications

Few offshore companies will venture even a budgetary quotation until they have a very clear understanding of the customer's requirements. In the same situation, many domestic suppliers might offer some figure, relying on the jargon of its industry to interpret a vague specification and secure in the knowledge that a written contract would be needed to enforce any significant purchases. Both parties in the United States know this and fully expect the figure to change or "firm up" as the specifications are examined, or change as a result of negotiations. Pricing will follow only after the specifications are clear. If the specifications might be subject to change, that is, if the buyer would be willing to trade features for price, the objective might recognize several acceptable product definitions. Presumably, the supplier will have been provided with adequate documentation to make a quotation before negotiations begin. Trying to get home-office agreement on possible changes to the specifications in the middle of a negotiation in Bangkok, though, could forfeit a quick and favorable agreement.

Price
The price objective for an offshore purchase won't differ from a price objective for a domestic purchase. It will, however, require explicit recognition of many variables implicit, or taken for granted, in a domestic price. Common business practice, especially within a given industry, results in *standard* terms and conditions for most purchases. A domestic price of "$100 per thousand" may mean "$100.00 per thousand, ex works, deliverable 60 days ARO with overshipments of up to 10 percent payable, shipping by common carrier prepaid and billed to customer, on payment terms of 2–10 net 30, payable by check in U.S. dollars." The implicit terms probably recognize that reliable payments as late as 60 days will be accepted without comment, and that some preferred customers may also be permitted to take the discount without comment.

For a negotiation offshore, then, the supplier's price is only one element of the buyer's cost for the product. As in a domestic purchase, it will be stated in the context of a specific set of assumptions about delivery point, currency, terms, and so on. Starting to think about these variables in the middle of a negotiation will be too late, even for many buyers familiar with an offshore industry. Constant changes in exchange rates, shipping routes and facilities, the development of local material supplies, or the growth of competition and many other variables that affect costs and schedule change as often as one visit to the next.

Quantity
From country to country, offshore suppliers' expectations and requirements for quantity commitments vary widely. A first tier Japanese company expects, and receives, pricing from the second tier and any captive companies, which reflects production costs at the highest forecast volumes but offers no greater security to the supplier than its name and a forecast. In contrast, the same companies sell on rigid quantity pricing and frequently demand letters of credit for any purchase. They regularly fail to order the

quantities they forecast to support their suppliers' best pricing but almost never fail to secure their own sales.

Trust, the prestige of the buyer, and the reasonableness of a forecast are as important in many countries in establishing the quantity basis for a price as any contract. Contracts or orders are virtually unenforceable in many countries or too costly to enforce. In many cultures a contract is simply a statement of assumptions; if the assumptions change, the contract is expected to change as well or is no longer seen as enforceable. In other cultures, written contracts are felt to be demeaning; having established a business relationship, the parties each expect the other to contribute to its perpetuation. Under such circumstances offering a huge order may have little more impact on a price than a well-researched market study and projections, a sincere and humble introduction to the buyer's company, and an honest effort to understand and respond to the supplier's needs and concerns.

Quality
Quality is not negotiable. Tolerances, finish, workmanship, color, and myriad other parameters are, and can be, reduced to measurable terms. "Quality" as a perception cannot be reduced to measurable criteria, nor can a supplier's performance be measured in units of perception. Compliance to specifications, or the penalties and required reaction to noncompliance, can be.

A buyer and supplier can negotiate Acceptable Quality Limits (AQL). They can negotiate who will pay the cost for handling rejected shipments, or the airfreight to replace them. The buyer can provide samples of acceptable and unacceptable product for the supplier's reference and negotiate for an agreement to inspect for them. An order can specify MIL or industrial standards and predicate acceptance of the goods upon the supplier's meeting the standards. A buyer cannot ask for quality without delineating the criteria and measurements that will be used to define it.

Procurement objectives should include 100 percent good product, nothing less. The buyer and supplier should agree this is the quality objective. Further, they should agree that individual shipments found to be less than 100 percent are to be regarded as cause for alarm and should spark a search for the cause and a plan for rectification. They may have agreed to an AQL level, certified shipments, or the provision of sampling data from a Statistical Process Control (SPC) program with each shipment, but any fault should nevertheless be reported to and evaluated by the supplier. The negotiating issues are cause and solution, but the "quality," per se, is not what will be negotiated.

Delivery

Both the length of time it takes for delivery after receipt of an order and the accuracy with which a delivery date can be set are far more important in negotiating an offshore purchase than a domestic one. Increased transit times are one of the negative aspects of buying overseas. The combination of both the production and shipping times, then, are an important consideration of an offshore purchase. Moreover, the order lead time provided the supplier may impact pricing, and, unfortunately, quality. Alternative modes of transport and alternative routings will affect the equation. China Airlines, for example, offers very competitive rates from Singapore to the U.S. West Coast because its flights are routed through Taiwan and the Singapore-to-Taiwan leg is often less than full. This service, however, takes one to two days longer than direct flights and shipments are often subject to additional delays. Similarly, several shipping lines offer "fast" direct crossings of the Pacific at premium rates, whereas lower rates are available on ships that stop at several intermediary ports.

Production lead times of the offshore supplier may also be subject to delays in obtaining needed materials. If, for example, the purchase is for an assembly operation, the component materials for which must be imported from the United States, Japan, or other advanced industrial economy, the production time for an offshore purchase may be very long, indeed, unless some means are provided to shorten it.

The delivery objective, then, is essentially a recognition of the cost of delivery time alternatives. The stated objective of the negotiations would, perhaps, provide that extending the customary U.S. delivery time by two weeks would be acceptable at a certain price, but that further extensions would need to be offset by further reductions in price.

A Range of Expectations: Target, Optimistic and Unacceptable

The set of expectations that define the product, price, delivery time, payment terms, and quantity commitment required to secure agreement by the supplier might be defined as the target objectives. They are, possibly, the assumptions used in a business plan or budget and are probably a set the buyer reasonably expects to achieve. They will almost certainly not be the goals expressed during negotiations.

The targets stated in a negotiation are optimistic ones, a set of expectations that are not merely a wish, but an objective around which a negotiating strategy might be built. To be effective, the optimistic objectives must be credible—a statement of product, price, delivery and quality expectations that, if not wholly substantiated by prior offshore experience, could at least be supported by comparison with a comparable U.S. source.

When negotiating offshore, the extended set of variables complicates stating the objectives while providing far greater latitude in justifying them. Do current U.S. economic indicators support establishing a particularly favorable rate of exchange as the basis for pricing? Do recent technological advances or productivity gains warrant concessions in offshore prices? What might the buyer's total costs be at a combination of the most favorable exchange rates, local labor rates, material costs, and shipping costs? Can pricing at this level be supported by reasonable arguments for each? Prepared, the U.S. buyer will be as well equipped to defend such positions as the offshore supplier. Unprepared, many buyers find themselves conceding issues merely because of ignorance.

The unacceptable, or worst case, is the point beyond which there will not be an agreement. The gambler who does not set a worst case does not know when to quit. The buyer who cannot recognize a set of conditions as unacceptable is in no better position. Being ready to break off negotiations if the best offer made is still unacceptable assumes the buyer knows when that point has been reached. Given the number of variables, hoping to identify that point without prior consideration is, in itself, gambling.

Naturally, there actually may be several acceptable targets. With almost every purchase it will be possible to define several cases of equal value, trading of some features or functions for a reduced price, or some adding of features for added price. The objectives, then, should at least recognize that the target product may not be attainable at the target price and delivery. If it is possible, or likely, that feature functions or appearance changes can be identified, target prices should be considered for each of them. Delivery schedules are equally susceptible to price, or premium, pressure. If customer requirements or time-to-market are critical to the program, acceptable cost increases for faster deliveries should be defined.

Acceptable Trade-Offs

What if the negotiations are not successful? Planning for failure is far from a negative or nonproductive exercise; it is a significant part of the negotiating process. First, and perhaps most important, it will help reduce the anxiety of the primary negotiation. Just knowing that there are alternatives strengthens a negotiator's position.

Next, and strategically important, prior planning sharpens the definition of the point at which the negotiator will walk away from the table. To determine this requires a little more work than merely identifying some alternatives to failure. It means developing at least a rudimentary plan and cost estimates. The exercise may also reduce the worst case and will certainly help reinforce the reluctance to accept a marginal proposal.

Failure planning also provides some real tactical advantages. If they can be discussed openly, that is, if they don't represent a threat to the supplier, the options planned in the event of a negotiation breakdown should be outlined to a supplier. The kind of failure options that can be reviewed include delaying a program, introducing a different kind of product, or redefining a product. The fact that they can be reviewed demonstrates they are real. The supplier will know that the negotiator has the confidence the options provide and will also know that the negotiator can identify the "worst" case with some accuracy.

Even if the supplier may not have a direct competitor for

the product, failure options represent competition for the order. To the extent the options diverge from the approach being taken with the supplier, as opposed to a replacement of the product or a shift to a new technology that the supplier can't handle, most suppliers probably will be quite willing to explore the options to save the business.

Failure options aren't new but, to the buyer new to purchasing offshore, they should become an additional consideration. In the excitement of traveling overseas, possibly after months of correspondence and preparation, tired and confused by jet lag, too many buyers succumb to the notion that not reaching an agreement equals failure. Active failure planning before a negotiation is the best antidote to this notion.

Supplier Objectives and Restraints

Trying to support a March new-product rollout with a hastily conceived purchase from almost anywhere in the Far East is an almost sure recipe for disaster; Chinese New Year's will inevitably fall right in the middle of the schedule. The typical U.S. buyer, geared to Thanksgiving and Christmas interruptions, knows the problems but doesn't anticipate them in February. The supplier, planning a vacation to coincide with the holiday, assumes that everyone knows when New Year's arrives.

Holidays are a small and unavoidable nuisance, addressed simply by exchanging calendars far enough in advance to plan around them, but they are reflective of the differences that cultural or economic pressures may have on reaching an agreement. The supplier's objective will always include profit and cash, but many will have other limitations that they cannot avoid.

Currency restrictions or incentives for payment in hard currency will preclude the supplier's serious consideration of payment in anything but dollars. In addition to actual currency regulation, many exporting nations provide financial subsidies to exporters, often by extending them credit at very favorable rates. Such subsidies are often restricted to certain types of transactions and would, for example, require a letter of credit to qualify. Suppliers that qualify for such subsidies will be very reluctant to consider sales on open account.

Political restraints are regularly at cross-purposes to both buyers and sellers, although marketing offshore is affected more often than purchasing. Japan's Ministry of International Trade and Industry (MITI) regularly provides "guidance" for the administration of international business. Voluntary restraints on exports may be a euphemism for restricting sales in reaction to U.S pressure but will nevertheless be an impediment to purchasing. Virtually every purchase from China is subject to political review, as is the salesperson. It is interesting to learn that the young bureaucrat handling a negotiation may be permitted to go abroad if a sale is made; the predictable internal conflicts are sometimes very visible.

Cultural or religious impacts on the supplier's objectives may be almost self-evident; the Moslem prohibition on doing business during Ramadan, for example. Other cultural values may be less obvious and so embedded in the culture that the supplier itself doesn't usually recognize them. The immense difference between the Chinese and Japanese attitudes toward individualism, or differentiation, for example, may be reflected in their willingness, or unwillingness, to undertake an unusual order. Few such restraints ever prohibit a transaction, but many do require some compromise on the part of the buyer. The customer may always be right, but inflexible buyers may never become customers.

PREPARING FOR NEGOTIATIONS

Ideally prepared, a buyer could irrefutably demonstrate that the optimistic objectives for price and delivery would return a handsome profit to the supplier, at low volumes and without compromising quality. More realistically, adequate preparation provides:

- a concise definition of the product;
- a good estimate of the time and cost to manufacture it; and
- some knowledge of the supplier's strengths and weaknesses.

Product Definition

As mentioned earlier, without a complete understanding of what they are expected to do, few suppliers will commit to a price or accept an order. Quotations or estimates that may be offered prior to receipt of adequate documentation will either be so high that they will provide a profit no matter how the product is specified, or so riddled with loopholes as to be meaningless.

If an offshore source will be expected to design and develop a product, it will need an unequivocal statement of functional and performance requirements, a precise definition of form and dimension, and explicit cosmetic standards or samples. If it is to produce to customer definitions, it will require complete drawings and specifications, functional test criteria, methods and standards, cosmetic criteria, component and material specifications, and, possibly, approved component and material vendors. If an offshore source will be required to perform any experimental, development, or research work, it will insist on a precise definition of how its performance will be measured. If it will be expected to use customer-supplied materials, designs, tools, dies, patterns, or equipment, it will want complete documentation of materials' function and performance and assurances of relief from liability if they are not as purported.

Complete documentation is especially important when negotiating offshore. If any of the information needed to precisely define a product is missing at the time its price and delivery are negotiated, the buyer runs the risk of an amended quotation. Such issues might be handled readily face-to-face, but it may be very difficult to renegotiate a price amendment for a minor change after returning from overseas.

Product Cost Estimate

Estimating the cost of manufacturing a product offshore is usually the task of amending an estimate of the U.S. manufacturing cost with the differences in cost at the offshore source. All three components of cost—material, labor, and overhead—may change.

Obviously, an estimate of the cost to make a product in the United States is necessary to do this. This means, at a minimum, a bill of material, including a list of material or components, the number or amount and price of each, and the time and labor rate of all the major operations.

Next, at least a general understanding of where material or components will be procured is needed to assemble an offshore material cost estimate. If material will come from the United States, or a third location, the offshore material cost may be greater than in the United States. Since the top 10 or 20 percent of the most expensive materials invariably account for 80 or 90 percent of total material cost, arriving at these figures will not be an onerous exercise.

Material source reviews commonly reveal any of several problems. Some parts may be tooled only in one location and new tools may be needed before the offshore source can produce without incurring the cost and delay of importing the parts. Some parts may be solely sourced in the United States or elsewhere, and additional cost will be incurred for the offshore procurement. The offshore source may be in a country or region where even common commercial components are not readily available, and any materials will add cost.

The labor required to manufacture the product should be examined the same way. Special skills or equipment that will require technology that a proposed offshore source could not supply may be needed for all or part of the manufacturing process. Proprietary processes might preclude moving the entire manufacturing process offshore. Very often, final inspection, calibration, or adjustment is not included in the purchase; this portion of the labor content is not moved offshore at all. It is not uncommon to discover that the offshore labor content of a product is less than half the total. This is especially true if kits of material are provided to the vendor or if retail packaging, including boxes, protective material, manuals, and other marketing collateral are added after the basic product is shipped to the United States.

A few other elements must be added to the estimate before a full comparison can be made with U.S. costs. Reasonable provision must be made for a source's profit margin and the costs of freight and duty. An estimate to procure offshore might appear as follows:

ESTIMATED OFFSHORE PRODUCT COST
Bill of Materials

Description	Qty. per product	U.S. unit cost	Extended cost	Offshore estimate	Comment
Part 1	1	$1.00	$1.00	$0.75	Cheaper offshore
Part 2	2	0.50	1.00	1.00	No advantage
Part 3	1	0.50	0.50	0.60	Import from U.S.
Part 4	4	0.25	1.00	0.80	Needs new tool
				0.20	Tool amortization
Total material cost			$3.50	$3.35	

Labor Requirements

Operation	Time in minutes	U.S. labor rate	Extended cost	Offshore estimate	Offshore rate
Kit, set up	10	$ 6.00	$1.00	$0.17	$1.00/hr. approx.
Assembly	40	5.00	3.33	0.67	$1.00/hr. approx.
Inspection	5	7.00	0.06	0.01	$1.00/hr. approx.
Test	15	10.00	2.50	2.50	Technical same as U.S.
Pack	5	5.00	0.05	0.01	$1.00/hr. approx.
Total labor cost			$6.94	$3.36	

Overhead Estimate

U.S.: Approximately 150% of labor rate:	$10.41		
Offshore Source: Estimate 200% of labor rate		$ 6.72	Very high land and building costs
Total Product cost: Material, Labor, and Overhead	$20.85	$13.43	
15% Estimated Supplier margin	$ 3.13	$ 2.02	
Total Purchase Price	$23.98	$15.45	
Freight and Forwarder's costs		$ 0.85	
Duty at 6%		$ 0.93	
GRAND TOTAL	$23.98	$17.23	

Supplier Strengths and Weaknesses

Among the most often neglected basic preparations for negotiations offshore is an assessment of the supplier's strengths and weaknesses, frequently ignored as an academic exercise of little value. In fact, without expending much effort to collect the information, such an assessment often provides a significant advantage to the buyer.

Has the potential source any exceptional skills it may be able to contribute to reducing cost, and therefore price? Does it have sufficient manufacturing engineering capability to modify the product for better manufacturability, especially in the country in question? Can it qualify for low-cost government loans for export business? Would local interest rates justify keeping safety stocks at the supplier rather than in the United States?

Determining a supplier's weaknesses may provide opportunities as well. Does it already have an international reputation and clientele or will it gain by an association with the customer's company? Will it gain any skills, improve its processes, or expand its customer base because of this negotiation? Companies that have never exported may be prompted to offer exceptional pricing to enter a new market; if their references included only local customers, they may be susceptible to such a suggestion.

Fielding a Team

A negotiating primer may suggest negotiating with a team capable of answering all the questions that will arise. When sourcing offshore this advice may not apply.

The advantages of a team are obvious: A team suggests the importance of the buyer's mission, gives the negotiation greater credibility, fields the experts needed to answer questions quickly, and may offer some tactical advantages in some negotiations. A team's copious notes can provide good ammunition in a negotiation if its members keep track of all that is said by both buyer and seller.

Team negotiation has several shortcomings in offshore sourcing, however, so a small company's inability to field one isn't necessarily a disadvantage. Furthermore, a team may be necessary because of schedule pressure and it will be apparent the team is operating under a deadline. A team that is too powerful doesn't retain the leverage of absent authority to otherwise defer making a commitment, perhaps to evaluate a competitive quote.

The cost of overseas travel also argues against teams when sourcing offshore. Suppose the XYZ Company is negotiating for 150,000 Widgets and hopes to buy them for a dollar less than they can buy them in the United States. The savings in going offshore should be $150,000. Travel and a week in the Far East for a team of five people will cost the XYZ Company at least $20,000. In other words, every trip the team takes will consume 20 percent of the anticipated savings. See Appendix 2 for further discussion of comparing offshore and onshore sourcing.

Is a team worth it, given the availability of facsimile machines? Are there any questions that can't be answered overnight, by the right person, from either Europe or Asia? Is the need for a team indicative of a lack of preparation? Given the additional cost of teams in overseas buying, will the advantages still outweigh the disadvantages?

It is possible to have the advantages of team negotiation without the cost and with fewer disadvantages. Negotiate at home. Create the understanding with any potential source that the expense of travel will be shared by both buyer and seller. Documentation, all the buyer's experts, examples of good and bad products, and failure analysis data will all be at the buyer's site. Occasional visits from a supplier will be worthwhile and lets the buyer field a team inexpensively.

Allow Plenty of Negotiation Time

It will normally take *three to four times* the effort and time to conclude an agreement offshore than would normally be needed to accomplish the same thing in the United States. To avoid the pressure and risks of having to negotiate under a deadline, plan for extensive delays in communication and clarification.

If language barriers must be overcome, the simple process of reading specifications and drawings will take more time. They will need to be translated, and the questions that arise may have to be retranslated before they can be asked of the buyer. Notes on drawings that U.S. suppliers may recognize as "standard" will be accorded the same degree of importance as the most important and unique ones.

Much time will be spent dealing with message bearers, not decision makers. Until all of the buyer's requirements are understood, most offshore sources will not respond with even a budgetary quote. Negotiations will not proceed until the source understands what is wanted. As the message bearers *by design* cannot negotiate, most attempts to do so generally result in making unnecessary concessions.

This situation is not uncommon. It provides the supplier with a strategic advantage in not having to respond to any requests until all is known about the buyer and what is being sought. The message bearers may not be the best people, merely the best English speakers in the company. The best people are probably in the supplier's home office and are probably the decision makers as well.

If it becomes impossible to avoid negotiating under a deadline, at least try not to let it show. Many suppliers will be more than happy to take advantage of a buyer's lack of planning or foresight. A potential source will be a little less willing to concede any of the minor points of an agreement if the buyer appears rushed. If the buyer must have an agreement before a deadline, and the source knows it, a premium will be added to cost for the commitment. Worst of all, the first round of negotiations generally establishes much of the basis for future negotiations.

BUILDING A STRATEGY

A strategy is simply the plan for achieving an objective. It can be very simple, and probably has a better chance of succeeding if it is. If the sourcing objective is the purchase of a common part at a low price, the strategy might be merely seeking a quotation from as many vendors as possible until the best price is found. A strategy to source an entire product line offshore might build upon a series of purchases, successively negotiated as confidence in the supplier grows.

Do not confuse strategy with objectives. Consider as many strategies as may be available, but do not plan to use any specific one. Without the cooperation of the supplier, it might be useless. Many times during a discussion, opportunities will arise to steer the discussion toward a planned strategy or away from one. If the discussion is on a rewarding path, do not change direction for the sake of implementing an enticing strategic foray.

If the objectives in seeking an offshore source include the potential for a long-term relationship, concentrate early discussion on defining how such a relationship might operate. The immediate objective of securing a product can wait. In fact, if the buyer and seller have begun to establish the framework for the long term, reaching agreement on the current product will be easier.

Identifying and reconciling the differences between the buyer's and seller's goals and objectives is especially important in developing a relationship. Some pertinent cases:

1. Typical American firms, and their buyers, are under short term profit pressure. They want low-cost product *now*. Their customers want product *now*, their markets are seasonal, and their marketing efforts are directed at this year's focus. They need inexpensive product quickly.

   The typical overseas source has built a business and cannot maintain it without its team of reliable, low-cost suppliers, who cannot react quickly and still maintain their low costs and quality levels.

2. The typical market is erratic. Customers want to place orders without much notice and to reschedule their orders frequently, increasing or reducing quantities on short notice.

   The offshore source has a small but loyal and well-trained work force. This supplier is unwilling, or local law would make it prohibitive, to lay off or significantly vary the schedules of workers.

3. The market demands rapid product change. It is difficult to forecast technical or cosmetic change very far in the future.

   The offshore source can meet cost targets only by making long-term commitments to raw material suppliers. Many of the materials utilized cannot be manufactured quickly.

Usually, the most successful approaches to negotiating an offshore purchase recognize the need for a long-term relationship. With few exceptions, few of the benefits of buying offshore will be realized in a single purchase. Following are a few strategies that have proved successful in accommodating the needs of both an offshore source and the customer in long-term procurement programs. They certainly don't represent all of the possible ways that supplier and buyer both can satisfy their needs, but they do provide an idea of the many ways cooperation can be of mutual benefit.

Rolling Safety Stock
This is simply an agreement to indemnify a supplier for holding an inventory of parts or raw material that cannot be bought quickly. Establish the inventory in anticipation of future demand. Inform the supplier that as new orders are submitted, the safety stock should be used to fill the order and replaced in anticipation of the next order.

If several products being purchased from the same supplier require the same materials, the risks in this approach are minimal. Identify the "common denominator" shared by most of the products. For example, if an alloy or chemical is used in all of the products, but modified in the process of manufacturing, stock the raw material itself.

Stock only the amount needed to bridge the gap between the normal order time of the material and the speed with which product must be produced. If it normally takes 12 weeks to obtain the material, and the supplier will be expected to produce in 90 days, an extra month's supply will be required.

It may not even be necessary to order or pay for the safety stock in establishing the program. The supplier, of course, will want assurances of payment for any that is unused but may be willing to carry a small inventory for a brief period at no cost. The greatest risk, therefore, is that additional orders will not materialize or someone will forget to notify the supplier not to replace the material at the time the last order is placed. By stocking at the raw material level, however, rolling stocks minimize a buyer's exposure only to its value. This technique avoids any commitment to the additional material or value added that buying completed product would incur.

If the material is expensive, or orders erratic, the supplier may request payment and handling costs. The only real cost to anyone should be the cost of money.

Mix-and-Match Orders

If the aggregate volume of orders will be fairly stable, even if individual products are not, it may be possible to satisfy the supplier's requirement for a stable work load without placing unnecessary orders. This approach will work only if a number of products will be bought from the same source and pricing for each of them can be agreed on in advance.

Mix-and-Match orders are placed for an aggregate volume of a number of products. The buyer commits to a total number of units at preestablished prices, over a given time. The commitment may be in the form of a contract, a letter of intent, or a purchase order, but its distinguishing feature is provision for changing the mix of product on short notice. Only the aggregate unit volume is firm, the mix being changed as the buyer's demand changes.

The supplier commits to firm prices, delivery response, and the maintenance of inventory to build any of the product variations in the agreement.

In practice, buyer and seller must work to define the minimum each requires to make mix-and-match work. The source will want some minimum production rates and adequate time to react to changes. The buyer may have to order some product in advance of regular needs to provide the source with a stable work load. The supplier may have to build in advance of orders to smooth factory loading. Both will therefore have some additional cost in carrying inventory longer than would be ideal for either.

Joint Product Specification

Many offshore sources could offer their U.S. customers substantial savings if the products they provide more closely recognize their capabilities. If the source has a reasonable expectation of continuing business, either long-term production or subsequent product orders, it will be very willing to suggest changes to reduce cost.

If the buyer's company has the time and resources to evaluate such suggestions, incorporating source-originated change into products can be very fruitful. Since many of the suggestions may not be feasible, owing to market or other considerations unknown to the supplier, it is necessary to monitor the process carefully. If the buyer's company feels that the suppliers suggestions are useless, they will be ignored. If the supplier feels that its suggestions are being ignored, it will cease making them. The buyer will play a pivotal role in the success or failure of such a program by ensuring that useful suggestions receive action, and by tactfully explaining to the supplier the reasons that others are inappropriate.

Transparent Pricing

One of the issues that perpetually nags both buyers and sellers is how much money was left on the table after a negotiation. A procurement process that simply requests quotes and responds to the lowest one that best satisfies the buyer's other criteria will never settle this issue. Buyers, of course, regularly test the market by quoting other prospective suppliers, but this approach has some real limitations. First, to make a true test, the process requires as much time and energy as will be spent reaching agreement with the current supplier. Next, given the inevitable dynamics of a company's product line, the price being tested probably won't be the same but, at best, an analogous one. Last, professional buyers have ethical reservations about exercising suppliers with whom they don't seriously entertain the possibility of doing business.

One fairly simple approach to the problem involves isolating the value of the material or services a supplier will be selling from the material or services that it, or any other supplier, must buy in order to do so. Transparent pricing, or supplier-provided costing, is not a common practice in the United States except in the automobile business. It is becoming fairly common in the purchases of assemblies offshore, especially if the supplier is providing little more than labor.

This approach is not new: Many businesses that transform precious commodities into other products build in "adders" to reflect increases in the price of the commodity. This is especially true of companies that use precious metals in their process. If, in this situation, the buyer were supplying the precious commodity, and the supplier supplying only the service, the supplier would have no reason to amend prices if the cost of the commodity rose.

Extrapolating from this business practice, consider focusing negotiations on the added value the supplier will bring to the product. The objective is to separate the various components of cost, ultimately isolating the supplier's contribution. Assume, for example, that a cost projection indicates that material, tool amortization, transportation, and duty costs should represent 60 percent of the total estimated cost and that the supplier's direct contribution of labor, overhead, and profit the other 40 percent. An increase of 10 percent in total cost translates to an increase of 25 percent in the supplier's contribution, a much more difficult position for the supplier to defend.

This is especially easy if the buyer has specified the product or is buying similar products and is already familiar with the materials and processes involved. Establish as "given," or at least subject to separate discussion, any material that is generally available on the open market. Exclude tooling and any other costs that could be amortized over time or volume. Plan to incorporate freight, duty, and other costs associated with transporting the product at their actual costs. Only a few of the cost components remain open for negotiation.

The strategy of transparent pricing is essentially that of persuading a supplier to open its books; the supplier's pricing will be transparent in the sense that each element of its costs are revealed. Ask offshore sources to quote in full detail, showing their costs for each purchased material component and to separately detail labor, overhead, and profit. Although a source may at first be reluctant to divulge its contribution in such detail, persuading one to do so should not be very difficult. Preparation for the negotiation should have established reasonable estimates of both the material content of the product and the prevailing local labor rates. The *buyer* can show the *seller* an estimate of the cost breakdown. If the calculations reflect an unreasonable overhead allocation, or an excessive profit, the source will be quick to detail costs. If not a complete cost breakdown, this will provide at least enough information to compare the quotation to others, or the buyer's own cost estimates.

A complete cost breakdown is a valuable tool. By agreeing to detail costs, a supplier will explain how the product specifications influenced the estimates. The buyer may discover that many details of documentation, considered minor or almost irrelevant in the United States, suddenly take on major proportions in an overseas market, as illustrated by the following examples:

> For many years Singapore had limited capability to texture plastic injection molding tools for certain patterns or finishes common in the United States. Specifying these textures meant significant added cost and time, because the tools would have to be sent to Japan or the United States for texturing. In both countries tooling is much more expensive and takes longer than it would in Singapore. In addition, the Singapore suppliers would add greater contingency factors to their quoted costs and schedules. When the costs were known, it became apparent that other ways of achieving the desired texture might be better. Providing samples for approximation, rather than specifying a rigid standard, was both faster and cheaper.

> Another example: The Pantone Matching System (PMS) of specifying colors for printed material is not widely used overseas. Artwork or film specifying PMS colors will be quoted at higher cost than if the colors are presented as "representative" with a request to provide samples for approval.

By explaining in detail the reasons for the cost estimates, an offshore source may reveal many areas where cost may be reduced without compromising quality. Moreover, in negotiating at this level of detail, a source can help reduce cost without merely conceding profit. Transparent pricing should become a major part of building a buyer-source partnership as well. By isolating the cost factors to which a source contributes, and the source's profit and overhead, both buyer and seller can work together to reduce any other cost without either giving anything away.

Last, transparent pricing provides several longer-term advantages in a relationship with a source. It will establish the basis for costing future orders and provide the means to forecast the outcome of subsequent negotiations. With several suppliers on the same basis, it may be possible to cross-fertilize them with materials costs or approaches to saving labor.

Multiple Company Negotiation

A variant of transparent pricing may be available to companies whose products are composed of several parts or subassemblies, or involve several processes, few or none of which would normally be found in a single supplier. The approach assumes a product structure wherein all or most of the subassemblies are specified by the buyer. In other words, the buyer could negotiate for and buy each of the components separately and arrange for them to be assembled.

Multiple company negotiation involves quoting the entire assembly to potential assemblers and subcontractors as well. Select several potential subcontractors based on their unique abilities to make the individual components and several suppliers whose business would normally involve independent subcontracting as well. Tell each potential bidder the scope and intent of the procurement program. Inform each of the subcontractors that they are permitted to divulge any quotations already received to any potential supplier who approaches them independently.

The buyer in a multiple company negotiation will reserve the right to buy directly from any subcontractors identified, without obligation to the supplier who first contacted them. The buyer also reserves the right to independently inspect and qualify the subcontractor, pay for and own any tooling the subcontractor may develop, and participate in negotiations relating to price, quality, and delivery. The buyer may require primary suppliers to use any subcontractor specified by the buyer if, for any reason, a quoted subcontractor appears unsatisfactory.

Solicit suppliers and subcontractors to review specifications and drawings and recommend changes to reduce cost and improve quality, reliability, or yield.

This approach clearly isolates the supplier's contribution from the other components of cost. Knowing they are competing for the business, several potential suppliers will take particular care to understand the requirements and will be less likely to arbitrarily add contingency costs to cover specifications they may feel are unnecessarily restrictive or ambiguous. Significant improvement in cost and quality will often result.

TACTICS

Negotiating tactics are the techniques used to keep discussion on a strategic path. Following are several that might be used or, more commonly, encountered abroad. "Setting the agenda," in particular, offers a possible advantage to either party in a negotiation. If both have planned to use the technique, merely arriving at an agenda may require negotiation! "Target pricing" and "comfortable quotes" are more likely to be tactics the professional will encounter and are presented as such, although situations may arise when the buyer may wish to use a variation of them. "Negotiating with contracts" is normally a buyer's tool to set the tone or speed up negotiations.

Setting the Agenda

When traveling overseas, visitors are often met at the airport, or at a hotel, by one or two employees of the offshore source. Although this is generally a true courtesy, it presents the supplier with a real tactical opportunity.

The visitor will have arrived tired. A drink or two with someone to talk to may be more comfortable than trying to relax alone. Business, ostensibly, begins the following day. If the buyer and seller will be traveling to a remote plant of the seller early the next morning, such a meeting will undoubtedly be necessary. On the other hand, establishing the agenda for a negotiation offers an advantage to those who set the agenda.

Publishing the agenda for a meeting permits the choice of topic and sequence of discussions. Inasmuch as these can be tailored to achieve an objective, a visitor's tired acquiescence to an agenda can cost that advantage.

Target Prices

An increasing common response to a purchase inquiry is a request for a "target price." This is simply a request for the buyer to name the price for a deal. Target pricing can be both a useful tool and a dangerous gambit depending on the buyer's relationship with the supplier. Assuming that a negotiation is just starting with a new source, there are numerous risks.

First, target pricing ensures that the unprepared buyer either (1) leaves all the money on the table or (2) tells the seller not to waste his or her time because the target is unreasonably low. If a buyer is not prepared for a target-price request and ill-advisedly speculates on a number, say 10 percent less than the current cost, the error may leave a 100-percent profit on the table owing to low local labor or material costs. On the other hand, a ridiculuous underestimate will conclusively demonstrate a lack of planning unless it can be substantiated with clear and specific assumptions.

Next, responding to a target price without the detail that needs to accompany it may allow the seller to respond with the "norms" for the transaction. In the same way that providing a copy of Standard Terms and Conditions of Purchase provides the buyer with a simple vehicle for stating the assumptions about how business will be conducted, accepting a target-price approach may allow the seller to name the terms. It is very difficult to negotiate upward out of a target-price quagmire.

Last, target pricing focuses on price at the cost of a clear agreement on the product: "Yes, we can meet your target price but a better material than we assumed will cost more." "Yes, we can meet your target, but the tolerances shown on your drawings specify .005 in. and our engineers feel that here and here .002 will be the maximum permissible for consistent quality. Of course. . . ."

There are few ways out of a target-price corner. Therefore, instead of responding directly to a target, indicate that the source should first confirm complete understanding of specifications. Alternatively, first express the assumptions about the product and terms, and then couch a target price in terms that provide an escape if mutual understanding is not found to exist else-where.

Target prices can be useful and meaningful to both buyer and seller if both already understand and have dealt with its implications. Knowing that the target price is really a reasoned one, and that the market expects product in the stated range, the source may accept, offer alternative solutions, or may even introduce another supplier. The partnership relationship will not suffer from a mutual understanding of target pricing.

Comfortable Quotes

The unwary buyer may also build a box around the negotiations by providing a prospective supplier with just enough information to quote a price, but leave the rest of the terms and conditions to the supplier. The situation is analogous to setting a target price with no accompanying detail. The supplier will be establishing the norms and setting the preliminary standards for quality, materials, workmanship, and any other variable the buyer failed to supply.

The source will have provided a figure with which it can be assured of a profit no matter how rigorous the terms, tolerances, standards, and quality level are. Moreover, as the buyer presents the actual specifications for all of these, the supplier can state that the assumptions of the quote were not as stringent, forcing the buyer to defend each expectation from being used as a reason of a price increase.

Failing to avoid being put in this position, there are a couple of escapes. If the quotation is not in line with the procurement objectives, ignore the quotation. Respond that the source may not have understood the requirements. Return to basics by turning the discussion to a review of the details of the inquiry.

Negotiating with Contracts

On the back of most purchase orders, in fine print, are the buyer's "Standard Terms and Conditions of Purchase." They are normally slanted in favor of the buyer. Most quotation forms, too, have suppliers' terms and conditions of sale. Most people have never read either. They can be an important tool in offshore negotiation.

1. Standard Conditions can be used to set the "norms" for a discussion. The text on most orders reflect Uniform Commercial Code expectations of the buyers' and suppliers' duties and responsibilities to each other. Most of the world recognizes that the United States has a well-defined set of standard business practices. Give a copy of a standard order form to the prospective overseas suppliers. Tell them that some of the text will not be applicable to international business or may not be applicable to the business at hand but should otherwise reflect how business will be conducted.

2. Standard Conditions can also help to avoid spending valuable meeting time over most of the issues they address. Invite a prospective source's perusal of the text. Since such a document may seem forbidding for someone whose primary language is not English, the opportunity to review the language at leisure will be appreciated. Responses will normally reflect agreement on many of the items. Buyer and seller will have reached agreement on many issues of importance without either party having to spend a great deal of time on them at the table.

3. Standard Conditions may identify some areas of disagreement that otherwise would not have been raised. Resolving any such differences early in a negotiation is far better than discovering them later and in perhaps less amicable circumstances.

A standard supplier agreement or a contract drawn for a previous purchase can also be used in much the same way as the standard terms of a purchase order. It can also bog down discussions in detail or create suspicion.

A long agreement may be frightening to many offshore suppliers. The United States has a reputation of being highly legalistic and litigious. Presenting a thick contract at the beginning of a discussion may make a buyer appear more concerned with the legal aspects of the negotiations than the business issues.

Few people enjoy the prospect of reviewing all of a long contract, but it will probably be necessary offshore. Don't feel insulted if a supplier insists on questioning every paragraph. In all likelihood it is the document that is distrusted, not the negotiator. Presented the wrong way, or at the wrong time, a contract may also lead to having to argue every point. To avoid this, make sure the issue of a contract is raised so that it does not appear threatening. Both the standard terms and conditions of a purchase order and a draft contract can be regarded as vehicles to eliminate trivia. Review any draft agreement and try to isolate the topics that will require discussion. Many of the issues in an agreement address situations that neither buyer nor seller want to be considered normal—bankruptcy of one party, disaster or war, disputes that cannot be resolved amicably, and so on. Express a desire to concentrate on the business issues with the expectation of a long relationship and, later, cover the more remote possibilities that could arise.

TABLE MANNERS

Listen

Among the first, and most often taken for granted, admonitions of the negotiating primers is "listen" and "wait your turn." Even if these appear to be among the basics that should have been learned in kindergarten, they are both very important to negotiating offshore. Just listening allows the listener to collect information and helps avoid disagreement by allowing an adversary time to explain objections, propose alternatives, or even just cool off. In the context of intercultural negotiations, listening takes on even greater importance. Offshore negotiations will be in English except for the meager few percent of Americans who are fluent in another language. In addition to the very cogent reasons for listening when everyone speaks the same language, mistranslation or misinterpretation now enter into the list of areas for disagreement.

If a potential supplier did not understand a question, did not understand a drawing or specification, or did not have either correctly translated, buyer and seller cannot know whether they have agreement. If the buyer and seller cannot understand the response or it was not correctly translated or the supplier answered the wrong question, they'll never know.

The injunction to listen is especially important when negotiating offshore. A buyer must confirm to the satisfaction of everyone at the table that every question was understood, and that every specification is understood, and that every response was understood. Watch for the signs that indicate confusion or misunderstanding; one member of the supplier's contingent may ask for an explanation, may object where an objection is inappropriate, or may point to a drawing or paragraph other than the one under discussion.

Wait Your Turn

The relative importance of time is one of the most significant cultural differences Americans encounter overseas. Not without some justification, Americans are known as being rather hasty, often to their disadvantage. In many countries, any amount of time that is necessary to consider and formulate a response to a question or proposal is acceptable. Too often, an American, misinterpreting a long delay as a rejection, blurts out an unnecessary concession.

Another disconcerting habit in conversation is that of "filling in" for someone who speaks slowly or just filling a void of silence with words. Both of these can be costly, not to mention discourteous.

First, dispose of filling in. Anticipating a response may be possible with a spouse or close friend and may often appear possible between speakers within the same culture. Across a cultural barrier, however, it is difficult, if not impossible, because the patterns of thinking are so often very different.

Next, common courtesy should demand time for anyone to answer a question. Allow extra time if the question needed translation and even more time if the response must be a particularly well-reasoned one, as many in a delicate negotiation will be.

Smart negotiators will use the time to confer among themselves. It is possible to create time with a break for coffee or the biological pressures negotiations seem to engender. The negotiator should express understanding that the question may pose problems and make adequate time for a considered response.

A couple of corollaries to listening attentively and remaining silent until a question is answered are particularly applicable when a member of a offshore source's delegation is acting as a translator. More often than not, this person is not a translator at all but merely the best English speaker the source can bring to the table.

Ask one question at a time. For many people this apparently isn't as easy as it sounds. Many Americans tend to embed two or more questions in the same sentence. In addition to adding to the possibility of confusion, multiple questions may not translate readily. Expanding upon this, try to keep only one point on the table at a time. Reach closure on every question and answer. Reach closure on every topic of discussion. Don't proceed unless the negotiators have either reached a conclusion or agreed not to do so.

In concluding a topic or closing a question: Don't assume that no answer is assent. Don't assume that any answer is assent. Don't assume that a change of topic is assent to the earlier point in question. If an answer is not a possible one for the question that was asked, reconfirm or otherwise reopen the question.

SUMMARY

Because of cultural differences and the greater distances involved, communication and negotiation with offshore sources takes longer and is more detailed than in the United States.

Good planning and preparation are a necessity for an overseas negotiation. Travel-induced fatigue and disorientation argue for establishing objectives and planning negotiating strategy prior to departure. Forgotten samples or drawings can rarely be received quickly and such delays are often expensive.

Focusing on common objectives, long-term opportunities, and mutual benefits will help ensure successful negotiations.

Quick, cheap purchases are the exception when buying offshore; identifying win-win strategies and mutually beneficial cooperation will enhance the prospects for successful negotiation.

CHECKLIST

Objectives
Product specifications, price, quantity, quality, and delivery targets
Range of expectations: optimistic, target, and unacceptable
Options in case of failure (acceptable trade-offs)

Preparation
Product Definition
> Drawings, specifications
> Quality and performance
> Inspection and testing
> Packing and marking
> Shipping

Product Cost Summary
> Material content
> Labor requirements
> Local labor cost
> Supplier contribution
> Freight rates
> Clearance costs
> Profit/overhead assumptions

Supplier Strengths and Weaknesses

Building a Strategy
Build on common objectives
Rolling safety stock
Mix-and-match orders
Joint product specification
Transparent pricing
Multiple company negotiation

Tactics
  Setting the agenda
  Target prices
  Comfortable quotes
  Negotiating with contracts

At the Negotiating Table: Table Manners
  Listen
  Wait Your Turn

CHAPTER 5

HOLDING DOWN THE COSTS OF IMPORTING: SHIPPING AND CUSTOMS

U.S. Customs assesses duties of more than $4,000 on a shipment of electronics parts valued at less than $300. The forwarder, acting on behalf of the importer, pays the duty and invoices the importer for the freight, clearance, and duty. Since the forwarder's invoice correctly matches the description of the inbound freight, the importer's accounts payable department pays the forwarder. The anomaly is not noticed until well after the customs entry is liquidated.

A simple mistake had been made by the customs broker preparing the customs entry. The goods had been part of many individual shipments consolidated by the forwarder and a copy of a page of the consolidated valuation had been presented with the customs entry. Although the manufacturer's invoice was included among the documents, the customs agent assessed duty on the entire amount shown on the copy. Because nobody noticed the error until after the entry liquidated, it took more than a year to recover the excess duty paid.

Because shipping and customs activities will continue long after a contract is signed, they will account for a greater expenditure of effort than any other topic in this book. Given the amount, and often arcane appearance, of paperwork involved, they are also an often ignored part of sourcing offshore despite the expenses. Carriage, clearance, and insurance all imply contracts independent of the actual purchase agreement if the product is delivered offshore. The large number of transactions required for even a single shipment create a tremendous chance for error. Freight rates, fees, and delivery charges must be continually monitored, especially if volume discounts or tailored services have been negotiated. Changing global freight patterns, fluctuating fuel costs, and competitive pressure all argue for regular reviews of carriage agreements.

This chapter is at best a perfunctory introduction to the topics of shipping and customs. Given the complexity of U.S. and international laws and regulations governing shipping, customs, commodity control, and the host of other related activities, it only offers a guide to the maze. In practice, most companies sourcing offshore rely on the services of their freight forwarders and customs brokers to effect the movement and clearance of goods in accordance with the buyer's instructions or terms of a purchase agreement. Nevertheless, even those engaged only in the buying itself should not proceed in ignorance of these activities.

SHIPPING AGENTS: FREIGHT FORWARDERS AND CUSTOMS BROKERS

Vendor selection for such services as carriage, forwarding, and customs brokerage should be made with the same care as is used in choosing any other supplier. In addition to offering competitive rates, the better forwarders and brokers provide a range of services in support of the buyer. Importing involves a number of separate services and several types of companies provide them.

Shipping lines, airlines, and trucking companies actually transport the goods. Some of these own the equipment to provide multimodal services, for example, picking up a sea container at the customer's plant, placing it aboard ship, and delivering it by truck to the destination, all under the control of the same company. For several reasons, few small companies ever deal directly with international carriers. The cost of staff needed to monitor ship and air traffic routes and schedules, to prepare all the documents needed for international transport, and to administer separate payables for the services needed is often greater than paying a freight forwarder for these services. In addition, unless the freight volume is very large, better rates are generally available from forwarders because they contract with the carriers based on the combined volumes of all their customers.

Freight forwarders act as intermediaries between the shipper and the carriers. They will arrange for pickup at the shipper, book space aboard appropriate carriers, prepare and deliver documents and freight to the carrier, monitor freight movement, support customs brokers at the point of entry, and effect local delivery to the customer. Because of the amount of freight they handle, forwarders may contract for space on various carriers, ensuring capacity far earlier than their individual customers' forecasts and thereby securing favorable rates as well.

Customs brokers are licensed, country by country, to implement the clearance of goods through the local customs administration. They are expected to be familiar with both national customs law and regulations and applicable international law. Some companies, variously known as "full service brokers" or "broker-forwarders," combine the functions of both. Freight forwarders who are not licensed will use a customs broker at the port of clearance, as specified on the shipping documents, or one with whom some arrangement has been made if no broker is specified.

Selecting a Forwarder or Broker

With sourcing plans sufficiently developed to make a reasonable forecast of freight weight, volume, and frequency, request quotations from a number of forwarders and full service brokers. Providing as much detail about the freight as possible, request quotations for rates and schedules for both sea and air transport, clearance, and fees. In addition, ask each firm to provide details of their operations.

Many large and reputable firms handle freight all over the globe, but only two of their offices are of real interest: the forwarding office at the product source and the destination office. Statistics reflecting massive freight handling may not reveal that a forwarder had only recently begun operations in Latin America or the Far East. Other, smaller firms may have only a few offices but these may be located in precisely the area of the source and with large staffs having long experience in the region.

Given competitive rates, we apply a half-dozen criteria to evaluating freight services. The most important of these is the firm's operations. Look for evidence of experienced staff in both the shipping and receiving locations, the organization of material and document handling, and the efficiency of record-keeping and retrieval. All over the world, during peak seasons, shipments are delayed or off-loaded, through error or design. A forwarder's ability to locate and recover errant freight is an important capability. Although not a prerequisite, many forwarders have computerized their traffic. Buyers of a wide variety of products, high frequency of shipments, or goods from many sources may benefit from the added visibility computerization can provide.

The total volume of freight a forwarder handles at a given point of shipment is important. If the volume is not sufficient for the forwarder to have contracted for a regular allocation of space aboard at least a few of the carriers operating out of the area, then shipments must be made on a "space available" basis and may experience long delays during peak periods. Space contracts also help ensure stable rates. Seasonal patterns of global freight, affected by the movement of such diverse commodities as Christmas toys and crop harvests, influence freight rates and the forwarder's prearrangement helps stabilize them. Of course, high volume between the shipping and receiving ports is even better. Ask how many air cargo positions the forwarder controls from the country of origin, on how many flights a week, and to what destinations. Even if sea shipment is indicated for a given procurement, this information will provide a good gauge of the forwarder's strength in the country.

The relative size of the forwarder to the volume of freight being offered may be a consideration. Small, infrequent shipments may be insignificant to a large forwarder and receive little attention and less service. High volume and frequent, irregular shipments may overwhelm a small forwarder. The offshore supplier may have important considerations in the selection of a vendor. The proximity of the forwarder's facilities to the supplier may be more important than at the receiving location. Excellent domestic transportation services in the United States could compensate for a less than ideal location at the port of entry. Marginal transport facilities at the manufacturing location may determine the selection of one forwarder over another. The offshore supplier may wish to recommend a particular forwarder from past experience.

Request presentations from the forwarders that meet most of the criteria. Ask for their recommendations. The better forwarders are clearly experts in their field and will have helpful suggestions to improve both cost and schedules. Eliminate all but a few of the prospects and visit their local office. If possible, visit their facilities offshore or ask the supplier to visit and report observations. Expect a clean, neat warehouse and an efficient office. Make allowance for the prodigious amount of paper such a business generates but look for good organization.

If no firm clearly meets all the criteria of the sourcing plan, or more than one appears to, consider a trial period. State the intention of selecting a vendor based on performance for a limited period. Monitor the forwarder's performance during the trial. Review the results with the selected vendor after the trial to ensure that the performance continues at the same level as during the trial.

Consolidation

The greatest benefit of using a forwarder is sharing the cost of transporting freight in container loads with other shippers. Except for chartering, the least cost method of transport is in sea containers, or airfreight "igloos." Forwarders contract to move freight for a number of customers who together ship enough to fill a container or igloo on a consistent basis. Further, forwarders can make commitments to the carriers to move consistent volumes of freight with a high degree of confidence. The carriers in turn, for the stability that long-term commitments for stable volumes of freight affords their business, offer substantial discounts to the forwarder. Occasional shippers cannot achieve the savings of the combination of volume commitments and container loads.

The forwarder also saves the carrier a great deal of paper handling. To the carrier, a consolidated shipment appears as one set of documents. The forwarder, of course, must maintain the individual identities of the customers' freight but this documentation is irrelevant to the carrier, to which only a single container is consigned. In recognition of the forwarder's role in international traffic, both the Forwarder's Cargo Receipt or Forwarder's Certificate of Receipt (FCR) and "House" Bill of Lading (HBL) or "House" Air Waybill (HAWB) are acceptable documentation of shipment for a letter of credit, if specified.

Consolidating has one major disadvantage. Because the freight of a number of separate shippers is combined by the forwarder, additional time is needed to consolidate the shipment at the point of departure and to sort the shipment upon arrival. This is especially true with sea shipments where unconsolidated containers are off-loaded onto trucks and pass through customs almost immediately. The consolidations are made available to the forwarders as they are unloaded and the sorting or "break-bulk" is done on a first in–first out basis. Allow as much as 7 to 10 days for consolidated shipments to clear customs because of break-bulk delays.

INCOTERMS

The many modes of transport that forwarders can offer will reveal a number of options unfamiliar to most domestic buyers. In addition to the familiar "Free on Board" (FOB) or "Cost, Insurance, and Freight" (CIF), a number of other terms exist and new ones have been added to reflect new modes of freight and other options. An international standard set of freight modes, "*Incoterms*," which were first published by the International Chamber of Commerce in 1936 to promote common understanding of trade terms, are generally accepted worldwide.

Incoterms serve several purposes. Principally, they clearly define the point at which delivery occurs. In a broader sense, therefore, they indicate the responsibilities and risks of both parties to a purchase transaction. In a brief acronym they reflect who has the duty to pack the goods, obtain import or export licenses, and what documents must be prepared. Incoterms also indicate where and with whom the risk of loss lies during the transportation of the goods.

Consider the many times freight may be handled and the many movements possible during international transport. Each stage represents a cost and the potential for loss or damage. The Incoterms cover the variety of points at which the shipper is considered to have fulfilled an obligation to deliver the goods. From "Ex Works" (EXW), at the seller's premises, to "Delivered, Duty Paid" (DDP) to the buyer, the Incoterms are as follows:

Ex Works (EXW).   The goods are made available by the seller for pick-up by the buyer. Since the seller is not responsible even for loading the goods, the buyer bears the full cost and risk of transport.

Free Carrier (FCA).   The seller is responsible to deliver the goods to a carrier. The term was created to recognize modern multimodal means of transport, which may provide for trailer/train or trailer/ferry traffic. The point at which the delivery is to be made must be agreed on by the buyer and seller.

Free Alongside Ship (FAS).   The seller is required to deliver the goods to the point where they can be loaded. Making them available at the ship, rather than on the ship implies that the buyer is required to clear the goods for export.

Free on Board (FOB).   The seller is responsible to have the goods loaded aboard ship at a port agreed by the buyer and seller.

Cost and Freight (CFR).   The seller is responsible for delivery of the goods to a named port. Unlike the preceding terms, the cost and risk do not coincide with the point of delivery. The seller is responsible for the cost of freight, but the buyer assumes the risk of loss as soon as the goods are loaded aboard ship.

Cost, Insurance, and Freight (CIF).   The seller is responsible for both the costs of freight and the cost of insuring the

FIGURE 5–1
Shipping and Customs: Seller's and Buyer's Costs and Risks

SELLER'S RISK AND COST   *BUYER'S RISK AND COST*

Ex Works (EXW)
Shipper supplies goods   *Shipper's*   The buyer's maximum obligation: all cost and risk to
at its own premises   *Dock*   destination, including loading at Shipper's Dock.

↓

Free Carrier (FRC)
Shipper Delivers goods to   *Local*   Buyer's cost and risk to final
a carrier at a named point.   *Cartage*   destination after the first carrier
                                                      accepts the goods.

Free Carrier (FCA)   The Forward qualifies as a carrier
Freight, Carriage and Insurance   under FCA and CIP. Buyer bears all
(CIP) to a named point. Sellers   *Forwarder*   costs and risks after the carrier or
bear cost.   forwarder accepts the freight.

↓

Free Alongside (FAS) Delivered   Buyer's responsibility to obtain export
by Seller to carrier uncleared for   *Export*   clearance for these and all preceding
Export   *Clearance*   modes. Buyer's cost and risk to
                                                      destination thereafter.

↓

Free on Board (FOB)   Buyer's cost and Risk to destination.
Sellers cost and risk to obtain export *Air or*
documents for these and succeeding   *Sea*
modes, and for loading aboard ship.   *Vessel*

↓

Cost & Freight (CFR)   The buyer bears the risk during transit
Cost, Insurance & Freight (CIF) The   *In*   under C&F and CIF, including unloading,
seller bears the cost, but not the risk, to *Transit* unless C&F or CIF "Landed" or
the Port of Entry.   "Rendered" is stated.

↓

Delivered Ex Ship (DES)   Buyer's cost and risk to unload
Sellers cost and risk is to   *Sea*   the goods, effect Customs
deliver the goods on board the   *Vessel*   clearance and delivery
ship at the port of destination

↓

Freight, Carriage & Insurance (CIP)   Under Carriage Paid To (CPT)
Seller pays Freight, Carriage (and   *Destination*   Buyer bears risk of loss after
Insurance) including unloading   *Dock*   the goods are delivered to the
                                                      first carrier.

↓

Delivered Ex Quay (DEQ)   Buyer's responsibility to
Delivered at Frontier (DAF)   clear goods for import, as in
Sellers cost and risk to Deliver to   *Customs*   all preceding modes. Buyer's
destination dock, or at frontier. In either   cost and risk for delivery.
case the goods are uncleared for import.

↓

Delivered, Duty Paid (DDP) to buyer's   Delivered Duty Unpaid (DDU)
premises represents the Seller's maximum *Buyer's*   The buyer is responsible for
obligation: all the cost and risk to the *Dock*   clearance and duty, but the
Buyer's premises or named point.   seller for all freight costs.

---

goods to the point of delivery. Although the seller is responsible for the costs, of freight and insurance, the risk of loss is still that of the buyer once the goods are aboard ship.

Carriage Paid To (CPT).   The seller pays the freight for carriage to a named destination but the buyer bears the risk of loss or any costs which may be incurred after the seller delivers the goods to the carrier.

Freight, Carriage, and Insurance (CIP).   Another term added to recognize newer modes of transport, CIP is similar to CIF but implies modes other than ship. The buyer assumes the risk when the goods are accepted by the carrier.

Delivered Ex Ship (DES).   The seller is responsible for the cost and risk of sea shipment to a port agreed by the buyer and seller. The term implies the buyer is responsible for unloading the goods.

Delivered at Frontier (DAF).   The multimodal equivalent of Ex Ship.

Delivered Ex Quay (DEQ).   The seller is responsible for all costs and bears the risk of sea shipment to the named port and for unloading the goods. EXQ contracts may be written for either the seller or buyer to assume the responsibility of paying the duty and obtaining import authorizations.

Delivered, Duty Unpaid (DDU).   The seller bears the cost of delivering the goods to the destination but neither the costs or responsibilities of clearing customs or paying the duties or taxes.

Delivered, Duty Paid (DDP).   The seller assumes the entire responsibility and all cost and risk to deliver the goods to the buyer. Whereas an Ex Quay, duty paid contract still leaves local delivery unfulfilled, DDP names the buyer's premises.

SHIPPING DOCUMENTS

Under all but the first and last of the Incoterms—Ex Works and Delivered, Duty Paid—the seller will have fulfilled all obligations at some point intermediate between the seller and buyer and will expect payment for having made the delivery as agreed. Under a letter of credit, payment will, in fact, be made upon presentation of proof of delivery, the buyer having assumed all risk from the point of delivery. Since the proof of delivery or transport will vary as the mode of transportation varies, it is necessary to understand at least the most common documents used. This is especially important in purchases made under a letter of credit. Specifying documentation inappropriate to the mode of freight will, at the very least, delay the transaction and will probably add cost to completing the transaction.

The most familiar term is "bill of lading," which is issued at the time cargo is loaded aboard ship. It is commonly specified as a "clean" bill of lading; that is, no defect in the goods or packaging has been noted on the bill of lading. Specifying clean bills whenever transport documents are used is recommended, if only for their value as reminders to the carriers to note observed discrepancies. Negotiable bills of lading are consigned "to the order" of the shipper and endorsed on the back to the order of the bank that issues a letter of credit for the buyer. A non-negotiable bill is one consigned to a specific party with delivery only to the consignee. To take delivery, the consignee must produce an original bill of lading.

With the advent of airfreight, the air waybill came into use. The long history of seafreight, and relatively slow movement of goods, has led to identifying the point at which cargo passes a ship's rail when being loaded as "on board." Because the speed with which airfreight must be moved, an air waybill is issued when goods are delivered into the carrier's charge, not when they are actually on board an airplane. The document actually reads "Air Waybill (Air Consignment Note)." Because of this, many forwarders ask for additional confirmation of shipment and air waybills may also bear the stamp "Confirmed on Board."

The various modes of surface shipment also document receipt of goods for carriage with waybills representative of the mode. The Convention on the Contract for the International Carriage of Goods by Road (CMR) provides for a CMR waybill. By train, international agreement provides the CIM waybill. In practice many other documents are used to confirm receipt of, or the actual loading of, goods for transport. Any of the terms that require only that goods be delivered to the carrier, rather than specifically loaded on board a vessel, recognize the carrier's receipt of the goods as adequate documentation. In addition, if a forwarder's services are used, and particularly when freight is consolidated for shipment, the forwarder, not the carrier, accepts the goods for shipment. In this case, a Forwarder's Certificate of Receipt (FCR) or a FIATA Combined Transport Bill of Lading (FBL) is issued. The acronym FIATA stems from the Federation Iternational des Associations de Transitaires et Assimiles, The International Association of Freight Forwarders, and the document is recognized by the ICC.

Shipping Marks

Shipping marks facilitate identifying freight with the documents accompanying it. Because shipments may be handled by many people, many of whom don't understand English or who are illiterate or semiliterate, the marks should be as simple and distinctive as possible. The marks specified are an actual part of the documentation of the shipment and should not be confused with bar codes or other means of inventory control specified by the buyer. Such coding can, of course, be included on the containers but should be distinct from the shipping marks.

INSURANCE

Since most of the terms leave the buyer with at least some of the risk of loss, insurance must be a consideration in sourcing offshore. Several options are available, each of which must consider the possibility of a loss, the value of the shipment(s), the consequences of a loss, and the cost and coverage of the insurance.

Insurance is available from many companies specializing in

transport insurance, which are readily distinguished by the words "marine," "cargo," "transport," or similar expression. Most also provide surety service, a consideration we will address later.

Obtaining individual policies for individual shipments will be an expensive process. Although it may be necessary for shipments of big-ticket items that only will be purchased once, or for other one-time situations such as the movement of household goods, coverage is expensive because the risk is so narrowly defined.

Offshore sourcing usually implies regular traffic over an extended time. Open marine policies may be written to insure the entire shipment plan. The insured's traffic pattern is examined to determine the maximum value of goods in transit at any given time and coverage is extended for that value. The total cost is far less than the cost of insuring each of the individual shipments because the risk is calculated for the entire projected traffic and only one policy must be prepared.

Freight forwarders will arrange for insurance at a shipper's request. The rates generally will be higher than for an open policy but less than the cost of insuring shipments individually. Unless specifically requested, insurance will be obtained only for freight or carriage, not for goods being warehoused.

Self-insurance, a common euphemism for no insurance at all, may be a viable option, especially for large-volume, frequent, or low-value shipments. Despite the tremendous publicity surrounding air and sea mishaps, the industry is extremely reliable. Many companies have determined that the loss of several shipments would be far less than the cost of insurance for their freight program.

Discount Rate Delays

The most common source of frustration when sourcing offshore is the almost inevitable delays or miscommunications of shipping. Delays in-transit are fairly common. Exceptionally low rates often reflect indirect, sometimes seemingly circuitous routing. Many airlines offer low rates to shippers to use flights that are normally underutilized, especially passenger flights with intermediate stops. For example, a route from Frankfurt to New York through Shannon, Ireland, or one from Singapore to San Francisco through Taiwan may carry little freight on the first leg, however full of passengers it may be. To ensure high utilization of the first leg, a cheap rate for the entire distance may be offered. If the second leg, Shannon to New York and Taipei to San Francisco in the examples, is normally well utilized, freight may be delayed at the stopover. The freight may be off-loaded by the carrier to await a later flight and replaced by freight at a higher rate or under time constraint.

Business circumstances may warrant shopping for these exceptional rates. A delay of one or two days every now and then may be an acceptable risk if the price is right. Shippers who contract for these services should be aware of their limitations, however. During peak traffic periods, in-transit delays of a week or more are not uncommon, especially if the carrier or forwarder is not prompted to expedite freight movement.

CUSTOMS

An inevitable delay when sourcing offshore will occur at the customs barrier. All goods entering the United States, whether or not they are subject to duty, will undergo some degree of scrutiny by U.S. Customs. Generally, this process will add no more than a day to receive a shipment from overseas, most of which is spent by the customs broker in locating the shipment and preparing the entry.

A customs entry normally consists of the invoice for the goods, the bill of lading, and the packing slip. An entry summary—Customs Form 7501—will show the commodity number, value, and duty, if any, plus fees. Upon payment of the duty and fees, the goods will be cleared through Customs. After review and processing, which includes both confirmation of the information provided with the entry and extraction of data for national statistics, the entry may be liquidated. A Notice of Liquidation will be mailed to the importer, normally, within 90 days. Before liquidation, Customs may request additional information regarding the goods from the importer, or, if a discrepancy was found, may issue a Notice of Action, raising or reducing the duty or making other changes to the entry. The importer also has the opportunity to protest the entry before it liquidates if an error is found or if it is believed that the classification, and therefore the duty, is incorrect.

Customs will assess duty according to the Tariff Schedule of the United States of America (TSUSA). The schedule is a thick volume of commodity descriptions and the applicable duty for each. The "Harmonized System," adopted by the United States in early 1989, provides for common commodity descriptions among the members of the General Agreement on Tariffs and Trade (GATT). Although the rates may vary, pre-Harmonized System problems of unequal treatment of the same commodity among the members have largely been eliminated. In addition to any applicable duty, Customs will also charge a merchandise fee, equal to a small fraction of a percentage of the value of the goods, to process the entry. If the goods were shipped by sea, a harbor maintenance fee will also be charged. These fees are payable whether or not the goods are dutiable. The merchandise fee and harbor fee currently total about one-fifth of 1 percent.

It is the responsibility of the importer to ensure that the correct commodity description and tariff number is on the customs entry. Although a customs brokerage will certainly be familiar with the TSUSA, it cannot be expected to discern some of the subtle distinctions that would lead to one or another tariff classification. Moreover, the invoice usually dictates which description is selected. If the invoice is in error or the product description is vague, neither the broker nor the customs agent who examines the shipment can be faulted for an incorrect duty rate.

Avoiding Customs Delays

An "ounce of prevention" will go a long way in assuring expeditious clearance through Customs. A determination of which commodity description will apply should be made as early as possible and certainly before the goods are shipped. If the TSUSA is not sufficiently explicit for the uninitiated to make the determination, the two best places to get assistance are the customs broker who will handle the entry and Customs itself. Customs designates certain agents "Commodity Specialists" in each customs district and at the national level to assist local agents with difficult issues. Normally, though, the broker and the importer, armed with the purchase order or contract for the goods; specifications; and product literature, can readily find an applicable classification.

Improper or missing country-of-origin marking not only may cause considerable delay in Customs but also substantial expense. U.S. law requires legible, indelible, or permanent identification of the country of origin on all imported products. The very few exceptions include items so small as to prohibit legible marking or items that would be destroyed by marking. In these cases, however, the packaging must include the marking. Customs has the authority to recall from an importer all the goods that it believes have been improperly marked.

Intensive Examinations

For most entries the customs involvement is little more than a perfunctory glance, if that. Occasionally, however, an entry will undergo an intensive examination. Generally, the selection of an entry for such an examination has little to do with the entry itself but is part of a group of commodities selected for periodic review. At both the national and district levels, Customs regularly selects entries for intensive examination based on commodity description, or country-of-origin or other factors. The process is continuous, that is, at any time at least one commodity will be under scrutiny. The following week or month, the criteria will change. Several criteria may be in effect at a given time.

All aspects of the entry will be examined, even if the selection criteria is specific. The product will be examined, the invoice and other documentation reviewed, and the commodity description affirmed. If the classification cannot readily be determined from the invoice or examination of the goods, or if other questions are raised during the inspection, Customs may issue a Request for Information. The entry number will be shown on the request.

The customs official requesting information can check the

box of a number of standard requests: relationship of the buyer and seller, additional cost of packing, commissions, proceeds, assists and royalties, or the return of contracts, samples, descriptive literature, or cost information. Other information may also be required.

The Request for Information identifies several types of additional costs, which are frequently overlooked by buyers new to sourcing offshore. Such costs may include the cost of separate packing, commissions paid to a third party such as a middleman, and tooling. Duty is payable on the total cost of goods acquired abroad and failure to recognize these costs at the time of entry is, in fact, undervaluing the goods. If undisclosed, the entry would not lead to duty being charged for them. Tooling costs, in particular, are often overlooked. It is not uncommon to create new tooling at a new offshore source and to pay for it separately. Goods made with such tools would normally be invoiced without accounting for the value of the tool. Having been paid for it, a supplier need not amorize its value in the cost of the goods. Tooling and other investment needed to produce the product but not included in the price for the goods are referred to as "assists" by Customs and can be independently addressed as goods produced from them are imported.

Customs Bond

The importer is responsible for the payment of duty to Customs. In practice, creditworthy importers normally arrange to have payment made by their broker and remit the value of the duties paid at the same time that their broker's fees and expenses are paid. Nevertheless, brokers are required by Customs to reemphasize this responsibility to their customers annually and are also required to accept separate checks from their customers payable directly to the U.S. Treasury if the customer desires.

To ensure payment of duty, Customs requires importers to post bond for the value of the revenue. Bonds may be either for single or continuous transactions and must be filed before the entry may clear. Customs will accept a bond application up to 30 days before the bond's effective date to ensure adequate time for review and processing.

In much the same way an open marine policy will be written for the average value of goods in transit, a customs bond will be required for the average value of duty payable under entries that have not liquidated. Most cargo insurance companies will also be surety for a customs bond.

Duty Drawback

Duties paid to Customs may be recovered if the goods are re-exported. In both theory and practice this is as simple as it sounds, but the documentation is tedious work. Simply put, it will be necessary to prove that the goods exported were once imported and duty paid on them. Because recovery of Treasury revenue is the issue, evidence of the customs transaction will be required. This will mean resurrection of the entry documents and the notice of liquidation for the entry.

Next, it will be necessary to relate the goods received to the goods exported. As the imports will normally have been embedded in, or sold with, another product or products, good material control and bill-of-materials management will be needed to substantiate the relationship. It will not be sufficient merely to describe the export; clear evidence that the imported goods were used in the product and re-exported with the product will be expected.

The export must be documented, requiring both evidence of a sale and shipment of the product. A purchase order for the export and an invoice for the goods evidence of the sale, copies of the actual shipping documents, and export declaration will be needed to prove they were actually exported. Naturally, the goods that were exported must be related to the bill-of-material that included the import.

Having documented the import, payment of duty, and inclusion in a product that was exported, the importer can apply to Customs for duty drawback. For many companies, this entire process is often undertaken by a service firm that specializes in drawback, or by many brokerages who offer this service.

Export Controls

An export license is required for goods shipped abroad from the United States. This extends even to calendars and children's coloring books. As ludicrous as the policy seems, in the context of the intent and implementation of the nation's export regulations, it is neither silly nor onerous. Although offshore sourcing may never involve exports, it is more than likely that technical documentation, parts, or tooling needed to start operations or other material will, in fact, be exported by the buyer.

Under the Department of Commerce, the Office of Export Administration controls exports of commodities and technical data to all foreign destinations. Controls are imposed for three reasons: national security, foreign policy, and domestic short supply.

There are two types of license: general and validated. A general license is not a document but an authorization to export certain commodities under any of several conditions to designated countries. General licenses include authorization to ship to destinations not requiring a validated license (G-DEST), shipments of limited value (GLV), for temporary export (GTE), for replacements (GTR), and several others. Destinations are defined by country groups. Country group Z, for example, lists Cuba, Cambodia, North Korea, and Vietnam. Country group S includes only Libya. The controls for Export Commodity Control Number (ECCN) 7999I, which includes calendars and coloring books, does not set a value limit and permits exports to any country without a validated license. It is probably the least restricted commodity in the regulations.

With few exceptions, for shipments more than $500, the shipper is required to complete a Shipper's Export Declaration (SED), showing the applicable ECCN, the units and value, and the general license under which it is being shipped. The reason for both the general license procedure and the requirement for declaring the export is to collect foreign trade statistics.

The U.S. Export Administration Regulations, available from the Superintendent of Documents, details the procedures for determining whether a general license may apply to an export. The regulations include the Commodity Control List, the country groups, and the restrictions that apply to each commodity by country and value. It also sets forth the regulations under which validated under which validated licenses are required.

Validated licenses are issued by the Department of Commerce and may involve review by the Departments of State,

Defense, and Energy. For some exports the review may include COCOM, a 17-nation organization aimed at preventing strategic exports to Soviet and Eastern Bloc countries. Some commodities are tightly controlled. Nuclear power generating equipment, regardless of destination, requires a validated license. Virtually any exports to country groups S and Z require a validated license.

A few commodities—munitions, narcotics, natural gas, electric power, and some watercraft—are not controlled by the Office of Export Administration but by the Departments of Defense, State, and Energy.

Import Certificates

The member countries of the Coordinating Committee on Multinational Export Controls regulate movement of stategic commodities through export licensing. Since the committee's focus is on strategic commodity control, end user identification is of particular interest to the controls. To facilitate confirmation of the end user, many governments require the submission of an International Import Certificate from the government of the buyer before an export license will be issued. The certificate both identifies the importer and requires the importer to confirm that the goods will not be trans-shipped or re-exported except with another approval. When sourcing certain commodities offshore, it may be necessary to obtain an import certificate from the Department of Commerce.

A special general license (G-COM) permits faster exports of certain commodities to the COCOM countries.

MANAGING INBOUND FREIGHT

Miscommunication, error, and sometimes fraud can quickly drive freight and duty expenses out of control and wreak havoc with delivery schedules.

Several common mistakes lead to erroneous freight billing. Freight rates are normally negotiated with a carrier or forwarder through a local office, but the invoice calculations are commonly made at the point of departure. Unless the office making the calculation is apprised of a contract rate, it will invoice at the carrier's or forwarder's standard rate. The standard rate also may be applied even then, especially if shipments are infrequent; the invoicing office may simply fail to check for a special rate.

Weight errors are not uncommon. Many freight handlers will estimate the weight of small shipments, sometimes generously, despite the carrier's and forwarder's clear policies to the contrary. A pattern of small, but regular, overstatement of weight suggests an unscrupulous operation.

Forwarder's regularly arrange for insurance coverage, often under an insurance umbrella. Although not common, small shipments for which the importer has separately arranged insurance or that are covered under the importer's own broad policy, may be invoiced for insurance in error.

Incorrect commodity descriptions or erroneous customs entries may lead to excess duty charges. If the product description on the buyer's order, the description on the shipper's invoice, or the commodity selection made by the broker at the time of entry are wrong, the duty assessed will be wrong. If they differ, duty will normally be assessed at the highest rate and all subsequent shipments will as well.

Managing Shipping Charges

A continuous audit of shipping charges are needed to properly monitor freight and duty expenses. First, the purchase order itself should correctly describe the product for customs purposes. Wherever possible the purchase order should use the commodity description, or a generic description, to identify the correct Tariff Schedule number. The commercial invoice that accompanies the goods should include this description as well as any part or model number the buyer needs for internal control. If possible, purchase orders should be written to include it as well. "Flair" Model 210 may cause confusion: "SILVER PLATED DINNERWARE SET, Flair" Model 210, won't.

Consistent packaging, in even lots and, preferably, even weights, will facilitate checking the weight shown on a shipping invoice. If the product is always shipped with the same number of units in a carton and the shipping weight of each carton is known, the invoiced weight can be quickly compared to an approximation of actual weight. Incoming shipments should also be weighed periodically for exact comparison to the invoiced weights.

In addition to comparing the invoice, packing slip, and purchase order, the shipping invoice should be audited, preferably by someone familiar with the order:

1. Confirm that the rate charged is as contracted with the carrier or forwarder.

2. Verify that the weight used in calculation is consistent with the estimated weight of the shipment. Notify the carrier or forwarder of incorrect weights. If repeated discrepancies occur, weigh each shipment upon arrival and mark the packing slip for later comparison with the invoice.

3. Check the calculation of rate versus weight.

4. Confirm the additional charges to ensure that none have been added for services not performed.

5. Confirm that the correct Tariff Schedule commodity number was used on the customs entry. If incorrect, ask the broker to submit an amended entry. If the errors persist, the supplier's invoice may be incorrectly describing the product.

6. Ensure that the valuation on the shipper's invoice is correct and that the correct valuation was submitted on the customs entry. If the shipper's invoice was wrong, a corrected one will be needed to prepare an amended entry. If the entry valuation doesn't match the invoice, an amendment can be made with the original invoice.

Monitoring Traffic

Good traffic management, even in situations that are not likely to fall prey to delay, suggests monitoring all freight. Any arrangement with a freight forwarder should include regular in-transit reporting as well as status "on demand." If it is apparent from invoices for the product that freight is regularly delayed, arrangements can be made with the offshore source to provide an advice of shipment at the time product leaves its plant and the carrier or forwarder is notified of it departure. Most forwarders are prompt in moving freight, but with the knowledge that their clients know when freight is being made available, even inefficient forwarders will ensure that shipments are handled quickly.

Advance notice of shipment, by fax, with a pro forma invoice will help preclude entry errors the first time a product is imported. With the advance notice, the importer's broker can confirm the correct commodity number and prepare for the entry before the shipment arrives. Advance notice will usually speed customs clearance, too, as the entry can be prepared prior to the good's arrival. With multiple shipments in transit, a fax copy of the air waybill will avoid any confusion about which shipment is in question.

If any shipping mode other than Delivered, Duty Paid (DDP) is used when importing, advices of shipment from the offshore source and in-transit reports from the carrier, or both, will be necessary for inventory reporting. In all modes other than DDP, the goods in transit have been delivered as ordered even if not yet in the buyer's possession. For accounting purposes, goods for sale are in the buyer's inventory and represent a payable, when so delivered.

SUMMARY

Importing requires the selection and continuing management of a carrier or freight forwarder and customs broker. The performance of a forwarder in arranging and monitoring transport will be a significant element in the delivery cost and timeliness.

The many modes of transport greatly affect the cost and speed of delivery. Direct airfreight or sea shipment costs significantly more than less-expensive indirect routings, which may also be less reliable. Multimodal transport or consolidated ship ments are two of the many options available to the buyer.

Both shipping and customs are document-intensive. Much of the documentation needed for shipping is also needed for the financial transactions of a purchase. Errors are often expensive and time consuming.

Shipping and delivery terms establish where the transaction actually occurs in a sale and define where the buyer's and seller's risks and costs are assumed. The Incoterms of the International Chamber of Commerce are almost universally recognized in defining these points.

Clearing the customs barrier will be an inevitable step in importing from overseas. Understanding the roles of the customs broker and Customs, the U.S. Tariff Schedules, and ensuring clear and correct customs entries can help avoid unnecessary delay.

CHECKLIST

Shipping

> Selection of the carrier, freight forwarder, and customs broker; cost, experience, locations, staff.
>
> Evaluation of the mode of transportation; rates, transit time, consolidations.
>
> Establishing the buyer's and seller's costs and risks.
>
> Matching the shipping terms to a letter of credit.
>
> Insurance coverage.

Customs

> Establishing duty cost; the Tariff Schedule.
>
> Ensuring a clear and complete customs entry; description of the goods, copies of commercial invoice, seller, intermediate and ultimate consignee.
>
> Country of origin markings.
>
> Providing necessary surety; the customs bond.
>
> Recovering duty for re-exported goods.
>
> Exporting; export commodity control considerations.

CHAPTER 6

MANAGING PAYMENT TO MINIMIZE COST AND RISK

Providing for payment may entail risks as great as any part of the process of buying offshore. Terms of sale and means of payment do not often get much attention from domestic buyers and few regard either as equal in importance to price or delivery. Offshore, they are issues requiring understanding and attention equal to any other aspect of procurement.

Following are examples illustrating the three principal areas of cost or risk in buying offshore: (1) rates of exchange; (2) methods of payment; and (3) the time-value of money. Although these risks obviously were not managed in these examples, each of the three areas can be managed to reduce risk, sometimes at a price, providing the buyer understands and plans for each of them when buying overseas.

In the mid-1980s, a midsize U.S. company was looking for ways to enter the fine quality leaded crystal business. A search for sources focused on England, which offered high capacity, quality, and good design. Enthusiasts for doing business with England seized upon the weakening of the pound, which appeared headed for a one-to-one parity with the U.S. dollar and would, therefore, assure a very profitable business.

Despite signals that the pound's decline was an anomaly, notably England's successful restraint of inflation, a massive effort was undertaken to start the new business. By the time the program was ready for final approval and investment, the pound had appreciated nearly 40 percent against the dollar. The increase to product cost rendered the project unprofitable and unworkable.

A small electronics company opened a letter of credit in favor of a Taiwanese supplier that promised substantial savings on its electrical cords. Eager to reap the savings, the company imposed a tight schedule on the supplier and attempted to enforce it with the letter of credit delivery date. The supplier shipped the entire order of 10,000 cords on time and received payment. The entire lot was faulty. Although the problem was eventually corrected, the electronics company lost far more through missed sales than the savings represented by the cheaper cables.

Another firm farmed out most of its assembly operations into subcontractors in Southeast Asia to take advantage of low labor rates. The product was inexpensive but rather bulky, a combination that prohibited shipping by air because the cost of airfreight was nearly as much as the product cost. The additional time the product spent at sea severely limited the firm's ability to grow; most of its cash and credit resources were committed to financing letters of credit or were invested in inventory-in-transit.

MANAGING EXCHANGE RATE RISK

Exchange rates indicate the value of one currency in terms of another. For example, one U.S. dollar may buy 2.0 West German deutsche marks (shown here as US$1:DM2.0); alternatively, one deutsche mark may buy 0.50 U.S. dollars. Since the U.S. dollar has long been the world's most important currency, most other currencies are valued against it. A few currencies value the U.S. dollar against themselves; the British pound (£) is the only major currency to do this. So most quotations for the pound will be stated: US$1.60 to £1.00.

Exchange rates that are fixed are generally not a problem; floating exchange rates are, and most exchange rates float. Even among the world's major currencies, large variations drastically affect the price of goods. In the 1980s, all of the major currencies showed major changes against the U.S. dollar.

	1/2/80	1/2/83	1/2/85	1/2/87	1/2/90
Japanese yen (Y):	237.80	234.15	251.75	158.10	146.50
British pound (£):	0.4462	0.6179	0.8703	0.6711	0.6230
German mark (DM):	1.7073	2.3815	3.1730	1.9156	1.7140

Translated to percentages, the buying power of the dollar, if 1980 was 100 percent, was:

	1980	1983	1985	1987	1990
Japanese yen:	100	98.5	105.9	66.5	61.6
British pound:	100	138.5	195.0	150.4	139.6
German mark:	100	139.5	185.8	112.2	100.4

Exchange rates are *always* a risk for one of the parties to an offshore transaction, because a change that is favorable to one will always be unfavorable to the other. Nevertheless, there are several means to reduce, or for one of the parties, at any rate, to eliminate the risk. Among a number of approaches to managing the risk, few are solely, or even directly, under control of the buyer in any but the smallest companies; nevertheless, the options must be communicated to and addressed by someone in the organization. The use of most of these methods assumes they are also agreeable to the seller.

Seven Ways to Handle Exchange Rate Risk

1. Buy in dollars: Since the dollar is the most important currency this is the most common option.
2. Forward contracts: These are agreements to exchange one currency for another at a fixed rate on future date.
3. Hedge: Buy the needed amount of foreign currency at the time the order is placed.
4. Self-hedge: Expect to receive as much foreign currency equal as will be needed for payment in the foreign currency. (Limited to companies that both import and export and have foreign currency receivables equal to payables.)
5. Do nothing: This is a relatively safe option in many currencies, especially those pegged to the dollar.
6. Negotiate a stop-loss clause: Agree with the supplier to suspend production if the rate becomes unfavorable.
7. Gamble: In some other currencies doing nothing implies risky speculation in currency arbitrage, gambling, in effect, that a given currency will rise or fall against another.

The buyer's assumption of exchange rate risk varies from no assumption to full assumption of the risk.

No Assumption	Shared Assumption	Full Assumption
Buy in Dollars	Stop-loss clause	Do nothing
		Forward contracts
		Hedge
		Self-hedge
		Do nothing
		Gamble

Because exchange rates always benefit one party and penalize the other, there are no win-win strategies in managing exchange risk. Although the price of protection may be very small, there is almost always a price. Even when the purchase is denominated in dollars, for example, it must be assumed that the supplier has included the costs of its own risk-reduction strategy in the selling price. Because there are no winning strategies, exchange loss management is a cost issue.

Buy in Dollars

Few suppliers object to being paid in dollars. As the world's standard currency, it offers little risk; moreover, many suppliers must import materials for which they can or must pay in dollars, and they can readily self-hedge. Many will, of course, have other means to deal with fluctuations: quotations with very short validity periods or padded prices for exchange and other risks. Furthermore, many countries facilitate the various means for the supplier to cover the exchange rate risk. Many developing countries will insure or protect suppliers by various means, although sometimes only in certain industries, against exchange loss.

The U.S. dollar isn't always welcome. In the late 1980s, the New Taiwan dollar (NTD) became a convertible currency and began to rise dramatically against the U.S. dollar. Taiwanese suppliers, who had for many years accepted U.S. dollar-denominated orders with little concern, found themselves losing profits rapidly. During an 18-month period the value of the U.S. dollar fell from roughly $40NT to about $25NT, a loss of nearly 40 percent of its value. Suppliers with long-term agreements with their customers often found themselves selling at a loss. Those which had extended payment terms suffered even more and many companies simply repudiated their contracts.

Forward Contracts

This is simply an option to exchange one currency for another at an agreed on fixed rate at some specific future date. Banks routinely make forward exchange agreements for a fee and at rates that usually differ little from the current rate; in fact, the "forward" rate for major currencies often appears in newspapers for 30, 90, and 180 days ahead. Longer-term agreements are possible but, as with any insurance, the price of protection will increase with the risk, in this case the risk inherent in a longer time frame. The quoted forward rates themselves are increasingly unfavorable to the current rate even in the brief period quoted.

Forward contracts are generally available only for currencies that are fairly stable and regularly traded; contracts on lightly traded, obscure, and/or highly volatile currencies may not be available. If the currency is one of the latter, the cost of a contract, if one can be made, may be greater than the expected risk. Banks usually put a heavy premium on transactions that involve a large piece of the unknown. The cost of a forward contract on the volatile Brazilian cruzeiro, for example, may be so high that even if a forward contract in cruzeiros can be found, there will probably be other, more attractive ways to reduce the exchange rate risk.

Hedge the Transaction

Hedging is, essentially, buying today the foreign currency that will be needed later. Since it can be earning interest until payment is due, however, the purchase usually discounts the anticipated interest earnings in a transaction similar to the purchase of a U.S. Treasury note. The process and calculation are simple: An order for 1 million deutsche marks worth of machinery from a German firm for delivery in six months, given a *current* exchange rate of two deutche marks per U.S. dollar ($1 US = 2 DM) and an interest of 12 percent could be hedged for about US$471,700 plus the fee for the currency exchange.

- 1,000,000 DM at an exchange rate of 2:1 is $500,000 U.S. dollars.

- 943,400 DM invested at 12% for six months is 1,000,000 DM.
- $471,700 U.S. dollars buys 943,400 DM today.

At the end of six months, when payment is due, the entire amount is available.

There are a couple of drawbacks in hedging: (1) it ties up cash that might earn more if put to different use, and (2) the interest earned is taxable. Overall, however, it is fairly low-cost protection.

Create a Self-Hedging Situation

This option is much easier to explain than to administer. It simply recognizes that if a company is owed as much in a foreign currency, from an export sale for example, as it expects to pay in that currency for a purchase, it needs no exchange rate protection. It can merely pay the supplier with the money it will receive from its customer.

In practice, self-hedging is complicated by many factors. The simplistic explanation above obscures the many real issues that must be managed. The payables will rarely equal the receivables. Actual receipts will almost never coincide with the due date of a payment. Whenever the receivables don't equal the payables, the risk of exchange rate loss returns. At what point should the company add other forms of protection through forward contracts or hedging? Will additional protection be needed if the period of exposure to risk will be brief? These are not procurement but finance issues. Decisions regarding how and when to address them exceed the scope of merely buying offshore and will, moreover, vary with the size, skills, and management style of the company that faces them.

Do Nothing

As opposed to hoping nothing will go wrong, doing nothing to protect against exchange rate loss assumes that the risk is so low that nothing special need be done, or, conversely, the cost of doing something is more expensive than the estimated cost of any possible loss. Although the notion of a stable currency is arguably a fiction when it comes to making decisions about exchange risk, most international transactions are not individually protected, a reflection of the fact that the cost was not justified by the perceived risk. The cost of protection generally depends on the relative stability of two currencies; insurance is increasingly less expensive as risk declines. The cost of insuring against exchange loss is no exception to this rule. Nevertheless, except in agreements of long duration, in single transactions of very large size, or during periods of particular uncertainty, purchases in the most major currencies are generally bare. This is especially true for pegged currencies.

A *pegged currency* is one that is held constant relative to another currency. For example, the Hong Kong dollar (US$1:HK$7.8) and the South Korean won (US$1:SKw680), to name only two, have been pegged to the U.S. dollar for many years. Currencies that are not freely convertible, as was the case with the New Taiwan dollar, are often held constant relative to another currency, again most often the dollar.

Currencies pegged to the dollar have historically been fairly good exchange risks, mainly because they were used in countries whose economies were supported largely by exports to the United States. They have become less certain risks, however, as the same economies faced the growing affluence of other countries, particularly Japan and Gemany. Currencies are held constant by the governments that control them and are stable only as long as they are able to withstand any outside pressures to change. A pegged currency that has long perpetuated an unrealistic exchange rate versus the dollar is potentially a greater risk than one subject to daily market pressure, because, when economic reality finally forces a readjustment, such a currency usually shifts markedly and with little formal warning. Therefore, prudent financial management would assume some acquaintance with the pressures of international opinion on a pegged currency before depending solely on pegging to ensure against exchange loss. As a case in point, congressional reluctance to continue the preferential tariff considerations being given Taiwan focused partly on Taiwan's nearly $60 billion in U.S. dollar reserves accumulated during two decades of growing exports to the United States. With pressure on Taiwan to both make its currency freely convertible and to recognize its growing trade imbalances, the New Taiwan dollar was not a safe exchange risk despite being pegged.

A number of countries attempt to manage their currencies relative to a weighted average of other currencies. Singapore, in particular, has been fairly successful in protecting its exporters by backing the Singapore dollar, not with gold, but by a "basket" of the currencies representing its major trading partners. Singapore's national reserves, holdings denominated in U.S. dollars, Japanese yen, German marks, and British sterling are periodically adjusted to reflect changes in the country's trading mix. A Singapore company accepting orders in each of these currencies can be reasonably confident that, over time, the value of the Singapore dollar will balance most fluctuations.

This approach is similar to pegging only in that it recognizes the country's export relations. It does little to protect buyers in other countries from exchange losses in their individual currencies or Singaporean exporters whose receivables are denominated in a single foreign currency. Moreover, the composition of foreign reserves alone cannot stabilize a currency. Brazil, whose currency is among the most volatile in the world, also attempts to hold its exchange rate constant relative to an average of other currencies.

Negotiate a Stop-Loss Clause

Longer-term agreements with any offshore supplier must contain some means of accommodating changes in exchange rate. Simply agreeing to requote each time additional product is ordered is probably the simplest way to accomplish this; neither the buyer or seller is obligated to continue if the exchange rate imposes costs or prices too onerous to either. This approach, though, generally fails to take care of order and manufacturing lead times; either the seller or the buyer has to absorb the loss in costs for material or labor obtained before the rate changed.

Negotiating ranges within which buyer and seller agree to share the risk of loss is often an acceptable compromise. Remembering that one or the other will always lose when the exchange rate changes, it is nevertheless possible to agree that within a specified range of exchange rates the parties are willing to continue to buy and sell on the same terms. In effect, each is willing to admit that, up to a certain point, the deal is still profitable.

Furthermore, there may be additional ranges, both above and below the nominal exchange rate of the original purchase, within which each party may be willing to absorb some of the difference in the interest of continuing the agreement. Rather than enjoying all of a 10-percent swing in the exchange rate, for example, each might agree to returning a third of the difference to the other, the alternative being termination of the agreement, and no profit, for either.

Such a price clause might read: "Product at a price of 100 pesos at an exchange rate of $1.00 = 95 to 105 pesos. If the value of the peso rises above $1.00 = 95 pesos then from $1.00 = 95 pesos to $1.00 = 85 pesos, one-third of the benefit of the exchange rate difference shall revert to the buyer and, if the peso falls below $1.00 = 105 pesos, then from $1.00 = 105 pesos to $1.00 = 115 pesos one-third of the benefit of exchange rate difference shall revert to the seller."

Under this agreement there would be no change in pricing anywhere between 95 and 105 pesos to the dollar, the seller enjoying all of any gains from 100 up to 95 peos and the buyer from 100 down to 105 pesos to the dollar. Between 85 and 95 pesos to the dollar the seller would enjoy most, but not all, the benefit of the exchange advantage and, similarly, between 105 and 115 pesos the buyer would enjoy most of the benefit. In both of the outer limit cases, however, both parties have agreed to concede some of the exchange rate benefits to the other.

Gamble

When dealing in many currencies, and in any currency during periods of economic uncertainty, leaving a purchase unprotected may imply risky speculation in currency arbitrage, gambling, in effect, that a given currency will rise or fall against another.

Very large corporations, those with significant economic presence in the international economic community, can ill afford not to invest in currency management and would be remiss if they did not plan to benefit from their understanding of what influences exchange rates. For those with the wherewithal to acquire the expertise, to staff the research, and fund the data collection, arbitrage is not gambling but another business opportunity. Although they may suffer minor losses from short-term market reactions to unforseeable events—droughts, wars, or other hiccoughs of fortune—they generally profit from their exchange rate gambles or, more accurately, from betting on almost insider information. The small company that attempts to profit both from its underlying business potential and through currency arbitrage on its foreign currency purchase agreements is venturing into far riskier ground.

Despite a lack of staff for collecting exchange rate data, the small company can nevertheless react to the factors that cause rates to change. For example, differences in rates of inflation between two countries will usually lead to differences in the long-term interest rates between them. This difference will eventually be reflected by an inverse difference in their exchange rates, that is, the high interest rate in one will attract funds from the other and, eventually, the value of the currency of the country paying the higher rates will fall.

For example, if country A's inflation rate is 10 percent and B's is 6 percent, A's interest rate should be 4 percent higher for comparable investment opportunities. That is, investors will expect a higher return from their investment to cover the anticipated loss from inflation. The interest rate difference will eventually be reflected in a devaluation of A's currency against B's currency (and will usually be reflected in forward rates). For more information on exchange rate forecasting, see Appendix 6.

TERMS OF PAYMENT

Once agreed, terms of payment are free of the uncertainty of exchange rates but are, nevertheless, an extremely important consideration in buying offshore, especially because the forms they take will involve cost and risk for both buyer and seller.

Almost unheard of, but nonetheless verified, terms of payment might be like the following one appearing in a contract between a large Japanese manufacturer and one of its international distributors: "Presentation of a 90-day promissory note 30 days after the 10th of the month following the month of delivery provided delivery was made prior to the 15th of the month." For a delivery made on the first of the month, these terms equate to 160 days! At issue here in the establishment of terms is the notion of security of payment versus the loss of time and therefore of the interest loss before payment is made. The value of the preceding promissory note is that it represented a stronger claim on the assets of the buyer than a shorter-term claim on receivables, a 90-day promissory note being more enforceable than a 30-day trade payable.

Although the preceding example represents an extreme case, it is important to note that security is often as important a consideration in an offshore supplier's payment expectations as the length of time extended for payment. It should not be surprising that the range of terms in international trade is extremely broad and tends to reflect both risks of exchange loss and the seller's assessment of the buyer's financial strength. This can very often work to the buyer's advantage. Many overseas suppliers can literally take an excellent credit history to the bank, even if the payment history abounds in payments made 60 days, or more. Letters of credit at usance of 60 and 90 days or more can satisfy both a supplier's security needs and a buyer's desire for extended terms.

Letters of Credit

A letter of credit (L/C) is more than figuratively "money in the bank" to a supplier; it is *really* money in the bank. An L/C is one bank's confirmation to another that the funding for a purchase is, indeed, "in the bank" and available upon satisfaction of whatever conditions have been stipulated by the buyer. When buying offshore, an L/C indicates that the buyer has deposited or otherwise secured payment against an order. An L/C further provides that the issuing (buyer's) bank will disburse those funds provided the seller presents documentary proof that it has complied with specified conditions of the letter.

The documentation required to satisfy an L/C will include, at a minimum, copies of commercial invoices for the shipment and bills of lading, mate's receipts, or forwarder's certificates of receipt proving that a shipment was made. In addition, since an invoice and a mate's or forwarder's receipt is little guarantee that whatever was shipped actually matches the order, other documentation may be required; certificates of inspection, consular or chamber of commerce certificates of origin, and so on. Nearly always, an L/C will be opened in time for shipment on, or before, a specified date and set to expire as soon thereafter as the seller might reasonably be expected to collect and present the documents required in the letter.

Letters of credit take a variety of forms, each usually indicative of different degrees of security desired by the seller.

- Revocable or irrevocable: Revocable letters are rather unusual and contain conditions for revocation or modification usually agreed on by both buyer and seller. The more common irrevocable letters cannot be changed or withdrawn once issued by the buyer.

- The letter may be confirmed; that is, the sellers, or correspondent bank, may separately, and for an additional fee, guarantee payment by the issuing bank. Although few sellers would request confirmation of a letter of credit issued by Citicorp or the Bank of America, it might be requested if the seller, or its banker, did not recognize the issuing bank.

- A negotiation letter of credit does not name a specific correspondent bank but allows payment from any bank. Such an L/C would permit a buyer, for example, to buy a commodity whenever and wherever it was located without the additional delay of obtaining financing.

- A standby letter of credit is one that is expected to be used only under certain conditions, payment of an overdue receivable, for example. Standby letters are frequently issued to satisfy both a seller's desire for security and a buyer's insistence upon extended payment terms without the bother of an L/C for each shipment. With such a standby, a single L/C might be opened for the maximum expected value of a monthly shipment, for which the seller has agreed to receive payment 30 days after shipment. As long as the buyer pays for each shipment within 30 days, the letter of credit is not, and need never be, used. If a payment is late, however, the seller may draw on the standby letter of credit exactly as if it had been issued for a particular shipment.

- A revolving letter of credit can be automatically restored to its original amount without requiring an amendment or opening a new L/C. Revolving letters are restored either in relation to time or value. A credit based on time might be restored to its original value after negotiation of the documents for the first shipment, and successively restored for 12 equal monthly shipments. A value limit would restore such a letter to its original value after any negotiation, allowing variable shipments but always ensuring that the letter would be open for subsequent shipments. The difficulty of stipulating delivery conditions over the time a revolving letter might be used generally limits their use to buyers and sellers with a long relationship and effective controls.

Several other forms of letters of credit may be issued, few of them advisable for the use of a buyer new to business overseas. Transferable letters of credit allow the seller to transfer some or all of the original letter to a second beneficiary. Usually transferable letters are used to conceal the actual supplier or manufacturer of a product from the buyer but can only be issued at the buyer's instructions. A letter of credit cannot be transferred if it does not specifically state that it can be. Back-to-back letters of credit accomplish the same thing, the original letter backing the second, which is issued to the actual supplier. Buyers should try to avoid placing orders that might be filled by a secondary manufacturer against a back-to-back letter. Effective control of a secondary manufacturer, which is almost essential to ensure consistent quality over time and in any situation where the product will undergo change, is almost impossible. Prohibiting the transfer of a letter of credit is simple; if the buyer conducts a survey of the supplier it will be difficult to conceal a secondary manufacturer, effectively discouraging back-to-back letters.

A single L/C is not limited to a single form; a supplier may demand an irrevocable, confirmed letter of credit, for example. Obviously, several of the terms are mutually exclusive. A letter can't be both revocable and irrevocable. Since no specific bank is named in a negotiation letter of credit, it will not be confirmed by a correspondent bank as well.

Opening a letter of credit is simple. Virtually every bank will have an application form; even if it does not issue L/Cs it will have an established relationship with a bank that does. It will ask for the seller's (beneficiary's) bank and account number, unless of course it is a negotiation letter. It will ask what documents will be required before payment is to be made. These will include invoices and some evidence that shipment was made as specified. The buyer may also specify other documents, such as written certification from a third party that an inspection was performed, for example, or certification of country of origin.

Although an L/C is money in the bank to the seller, it need not be the buyer's money if the buyer has sufficient credit to cover the letter. The bank with which the buyer has a credit line will, of course, consider the credit line utilized to the extent it has issued letters of credit, but separate cash deposits won't be required. Banks do, however, back their letters of credit with bankers' acceptances, negotiable instruments representing deposits made at discount and payable upon expiration of the letters, or with pools of deposits that serve the same purpose in backing large numbers of letters of credit.

Note that an L/C requires only documentation, not physical proof, for payment. Invoices and a bill of lading for freight marked with the correct description do not guarantee that the shipment was made as agreed but may be all that is necessary to obtain payment. Neither of the banks party to an L/C has any responsibility to authenticate the documents that an L/C may call for as long as they comply with the terms of the L/C, and they bear no liability even if the documents are fraudulently submitted. More than one importer has a story about a company somewhere that simply ceased to exist after presenting documents for a worthless shipment. Although a buyer can specify onerous amounts of documentation, an L/C principally serves to provide guarantees to a seller. Confirmation that the seller will be a reliable supplier should be sought well before an L/C is issued.

The fact that a buyer can demand myriad documents too

frequently leads to attempts to use letters of credit as enforcement tools, a function they serve poorly and one that the International Chamber of Commerce specifically suggests avoiding. Errors in shipments, late deliveries, short shipments, and other failures in compliance will invariably plague even the most capable and conscientious suppliers. Such deviations are regularly addressed by the bank's party to an L/C; the beneficiary (supplier) indicates to its (the correspondent) bank that it cannot comply with the terms of the L/C and requests that it confirm, through the issuing bank, that the buyer will authorize payment despite the deviation.

Nevertheless, even experienced buyers tend to rely on letters of credit to bring pressure on suppliers to meet shipping dates, forgetting that an L/C is a poor substitute for a solid agreement between buyer and seller. Frequently, experienced suppliers of standard commodities will deliberately miss an unreasonable shipping date in the first L/C issued by a new customer, especially if there is even a hint that some of the delay could be attributed to the buyer, such as vague or incomplete specifications. Such a gesture clearly demonstrates the function of the L/C, protecting the supplier; it becomes abundantly clear to the buyer that at a cost of several hundred dollars per L/C, using them as enforcement tools will be expensive and subsequent letters generally state reasonable requirements.

Discrepancies between the requirements of an L/C and the documents actually submitted occur frequently. Normally, the supplier merely corrects the error and resubmits the documents before the letter expires. If it is not possible to correct the error, but the supplier feels that it has complied substantially with the conditions of the letter, it may ask its bank to request authority to pay from the issuing bank. The issuing bank will notify the buyer of the discrepancy and request for payment. The buyer may also request the documents themselves for review.

The instrument of payment for an L/C is a draft against an account opened when the letter is issued. Payment may be made at "sight" or at some number of days "usance." Payment at usance may satisfy both a seller's desire for security and a buyer's wish for extended terms. Although payment at usance won't permit stopping payment of an irrevocable L/C, a buyer may wish an opportunity to receive and inspect goods prior to payment, whereas other agreements may provide for remedies for nonconforming shipments. Buyer and seller must agree who will earn the interest of an L/C at usance during the period after presentation of documents and payment.

Drafts

Drafts are bills of exchange that can be drawn at sight or demand or postdated (usance drafts). They are not used solely in conjunction with a letter of credit but are, themselves, the principal instrument used for payment for international goods. A common check is also a normal and acceptable method of payment, but drafts provide more flexibility. The only variables in a check are the date the check becomes negotiable, the amount, and the name of the payee. Drafts can set additional conditions to be met before payment will occur. In addition to accompanying an L/C as the means of payment, several other types of drafts satisfy several different problems, like timing of payment, which are commonly encountered in international sourcing.

Sight drafts are drawn for the amount of the vendor's invoice and are payable upon the vendor's presentation of the appropriate shipping documents for the completed order. Note that there is no limitation on the shipping date with a sight draft, as there is with an L/C. Therefore, if the buyer doesn't feel the need for the constraints of an L/C and the seller doesn't require the security of one, a draft might be the preferable instrument.

Arrival drafts are payable to the vendor upon arrival of the goods, through Customs, in the home country. Arrival drafts solve, for example, the problem of an occasionally erratic supplier, or one trying to operate within a weak and unreliable infrastructure.

Time drafts are payable at a specified date and usually have no relation to the status of the goods. These drafts are often used when licensing payments or other fees must be paid periodically to the source for services rendered.

Documents against Payment (D/P) and Documents against Acceptance (D/A) are the most common means of payment with drafts. Under Documents against Payment, the supplier ships the goods and receives the proof that title to them was transferred, normally a carrier's receipt. Payment against the draft will be made upon presentation of the documents. Under Documents against Acceptance, payment will not be made until the buyer accepts title. Note that under laws of carriage, title to goods is transferred to the carrier when shipments are made, not directly to the buyer, providing the carrier leverage to exact payment for transport for the goods they move. Using either Documents against Payment or Acceptance the supplier assumes a greater risk than with a letter of credit, since title under both D/P and D/A will have been transferred before payment is made. Further, under D/A, the supplier bears the added risk that the buyer will not accept title to the shipment.

Note how the added stipulations required for payment using drafts differs from the use of ordinary blank checks. A draft can be drawn to require specific documentation as an L/C does but does not require that the cash for payment be on deposit when it is issued. In addition, unlike a check, a draft can be drawn to be payable a set length of time after certain performance by the seller, 30 days after shipment, for example, and its payment date may be effectively tied to the documentation of such performance. Although drafts provide no guarantee that funds are available to back them, they are nevertheless a stronger guarantee of payment than a check. The supplier will, at least, have possession of a draft before shipment, whereas an open account transaction offers no assurance of any provision for payment.

Open Account

Within their own countries, offshore suppliers rarely enjoy the payment security an L/C affords them. More often than not, local terms are far less favorable than the "Net 30" prevailing in the United States. The alert buyer can generally determine and postulate local terms as a "standard" against which other payment alternatives can be measured, arguing, for example, that any interest losses inherent in the payment form agreed on should be borne by the seller up to the standard terms for local purchases. Although this may appear to be little more than a negotiating position with little chance of having a substantive impact, it will serve to focus on the costs of payment timing and will lend credence to arguments for something less severe than interminable letters of credit.

Given mutual confidence between buyer and seller, there is little need for letters of credit. Certainly, a shrewd supplier will insist on L/Cs for the assurance and very favorable payment timing they provide, but after the buyer's credit and payment performance have been demonstrated, they are nice, but not necessary, for the seller.

It will nevertheless be apparent that the normal practice of satisfying payment on open account in the United States, payment by check, will probably not be very acceptable to an offshore supplier many weeks away by mail. Telegraphic transfers (TTs) or, alternatively, wire transfers are simple expedients to the need to make prompt and timely payments without the commitments required by L/Cs or drafts or the delay of mailed checks. Any bank, for an almost negligible fee, will transfer funds this way.

MANAGING PAYMENT SCHEDULES

The time value of money is simply what it could be earning, at interest or in some other investment opportunity, over any given time. As any business struggling to manage its receivables knows, the faster it gets paid, the faster those funds can be put to work earning interest or buying material for future sales.

When purchasing domestically, the relatively brief time it takes to receive a purchase after it is shipped by the supplier goes almost unnoticed. The supplier may invoice the shipment when it leaves its factory, but the one or two days transit time it requires still permits the buyer to use the purchase for a substantial time before payment is due, usually 30 days or more. The buyer may even be able to process the purchase and make sales of its own even before payment is due on the material it used. In addition, buyers will usually have time to inspect the shipment before payment is due and, if it is defective, to suspend payment while any discrepancies are being addressed.

Probably the biggest disincentive to buying offshore is the

length of time it takes to get delivery of a shipment. It is not uncommon for shipments to be in-transit for 30, 40, or even 50 days, especially if Less than Container Load (LCL) trans-Pacific, trans-Canal, or multimodal shipments are being made to buyers well inland of the major ports of entry. If the buyer's company adds further processing, distributes through a lengthy channel, or extends payment terms, it is very likely that six months or more will have passed before a buyer is paid for the sale of whatever it imports.

In addition, even if buying offshore requires only a short transit time from the supplier to the buyer, it may also result in much earlier commitment of funds than buying domestically. Buying with an L/C requires a commitment of resources at the time an order is placed, whether such commitment is the actual deposit of cash or an obligation on the buyer's line of credit. In comparison, no such commitment is made when buying on open account. A company that normally pays suppliers in 30 days must commit funding three months earlier when buying offshore against quoted delivery 60 days after the opening of an L/C.

Except to achieve really remarkable savings, few companies are willing or able to restrict their capital and limit their flexibility to such a degree. This is especially true considering that such funding commitments also imply the need to protect against exchange loss. Extending payment terms should rank high among the objectives of the earliest negotiations.

Getting Better Payment Terms

1. Reduce order lead times. Even under an L/C at sight, funds are restricted for a shorter period.
2. Issue letters of credit at usance. The supplier gets security even while payment is extended.
3. Do business on open account. If necessary, issue a standby L/C for security.
4. Get agreement to set off debits against future orders. If a shipment doesn't meet specifications, reduce the next payment by its value.
5. Take deliveries closer to the destination.

6. Move to successively better terms.

Reduce Order Lead Times

This is one of the few Win-Win solutions to the payment problems which arise when buying offshore, if it is possible. To the buyer it means tying up resources for a shorter period and a greater ability to react to market conditions, an added benefit. To the supplier it means faster production and payment, a better use of its resources. Reducing lead times may be difficult but there are several approaches which work.

Increasing experience in producing the product and growing confidence in the buyer will have a major impact on lead times. The supplier may be persuaded to carry limited stock in anticipation of orders, or, and more likely, it may induce local distributors to carry more stock once a demand has been recognized. More formal safety stock measures might also be appropriate.

After the first few production cycles, a joint review of the relationship will probably reveal several areas where improvement is possible, from simply streamlining the order placement process to major changes in the materials, processes, or specifications for the product. The value of such a review is usually enhanced by setting a reduction on order lead times as its clear objective, rather than merely "getting together to talk about our business."

Issue Letters of Credit at Usance

As outlined earlier, Letters of Credit need not be payable at sight, although the term is used so often it overshadows the alternatives. An L/C at usance delays payment for a specified number of days after the documents are sighted and still provides excellent security for the supplier, even in the case of faulty or erroneous shipments once the required documents have been accepted. It also allows the buyer the interest on the funds, albeit at usually modest interest rates and restricts them from any other investment use.

Do Business on Open Account

Once mutual respect and confidence have been built between buyer and seller, there is little reason business can't be conducted on open account and on whatever terms best serve the needs of both. Forty-five- and 60-day terms are not uncommon between suppliers in the Far East and their U.S. customers. Such terms are common among local businesses there and the suppliers, therefore, are not being asked to finance their customer's payables to any greater extent than prevailing local conditions. The U.S. buyer taking delivery in the Far East and shipping by sea is able both to take advantage of the least costly means of transport and still schedule payment for some time after arrival of the goods, often in terms essentially the same as if they were purchased domestically.

Set Off Debits against Future Payments

The buyer's risk of receiving nonconforming goods after having made payment, and often without clear recourse to the supplier, is one of the most frustrating liabilities of buying offshore. Even when procuring from reliable sources, handling rejects is, at best, time consuming. Assuming an ongoing relationship and continuing purchases, and clear agreement between both buyer and supplier on specifications, most suppliers will agree to allow the buyer to set off rejected material debits against future payments. The return, and repair or replacement, of the material is then handled as a new order and the buyer's funds are not restricted while the problem is being corrected.

This approach does have a couple of significant flaws: First, setoffs are unworkable if the supplier is factoring its receivables, that is, if it is selling them to a bank or other institution at a discount, ultimately to be collected by the factor. In such cases, the supplier will usually have sold the receivables to an institution that has no responsibility for performance under the seller's contract. Next, unless the goods may be imported duty free, or documentation is readily and easily prepared to avoid repayment of duty when the goods are returned after repair, double duty costs may be incurred. This is especially true if the product is a commodity that cannot easily be identified by serial number or other unique identification.

Take Delivery Closer to the Destination

Placing orders Delivered, Duty Paid (DDP) eliminates virtually all of the timing issues of payment, and many of the other issues of buying offshore as well. Although it may not be an option—many suppliers are not staffed or will simply refuse to accept all the responsibilities DDP implies—there may be room to negotiate point of delivery when addressing payment issues.

There will usually be added costs for deliveries made close to the buyer's destination. Increasing the supplier's responsibility for arranging transport or added documentation implies added staffing. Nearer destinations may also imply added costs for clearance, or duty, and any added responsibility increases the supplier's performance risk as it becomes successively dependent upon the carriers, forwarders, brokers, and customs. Few suppliers will provide the added services merely at cost but will expect added compensation for the effort. Estimated actual costs will also be inflated to cover contingencies, such as the need to make a shipment by airfreight to compensate for a delay caused by a sea carrier or forwarder.

Move to Successively Better Terms

No matter what specific opportunities may present themselves, seek agreement with all suppliers that, as payment performance is established, less rigid terms will apply; that L/Cs will be abandoned in favor of open account, or arrival drafts, or that a standby L/C will be acceptable. Establishing open account payment terms as an objective of the relationship early in the relationship may help forestall the supplier from asking for an increase in price, "to cover the lost interest," as better terms are implemented.

Seek commitment on terminating the more rigorous terms after a specified period and, if possible, include the time and conditions for such changes in an agreement. It might be agreed to substitute a standby L/C for individual L/Cs after the first three shipments and abandon the standby, given acceptable payment performance on the part of the buyer, six months thereafter.

SUMMARY

Paying for goods or services purchased overseas involves risks that are not encountered domestically. Either the buyer or seller must assume the risk that the relative valuation of the currencies involved will change between when an order is placed and when delivery is effected. There are no win-win solutions for the exchange rate problem, but the risk can be reduced in a number of ways.

A wide variety of terms of sale and instruments of payment, not normally encountered when purchasing domestically, will be encountered when buying in foreign markets. Terms may vary from strong assurances of payment such as letters of credit provide, to extended terms well beyond the 30 days common to U.S. business. A variety of conditions may apply to drafts or letters of credit, and, since the seller is usually the party to stipulate them, buyers doing business offshore need to be familiar with them.

Obtaining better payment terms from a foreign supplier generally requires addressing payment issues early in the relationship. Early notice of the buyer's expectation to move the relationship to terms customary in the United States should be given even if the first purchases are financed by letters of credit.

CHECKLIST

Managing Exchange Rate Risk
> Buy in dollars
> Forward contracts
> Hedging
> Self-Hedges
> Do nothing; pegged currencies
> Negotiate a stop loss clause
> Gamble; currency arbitrage

Terms of Payment
> Letters of credit
>> Sight or usance
>> Revocable or irrevocable
>> Confirmed or unconfirmed
>> Negotiation letters
>> Standby letters

Revolving letters

Drafts
Sight or usance
Arrival drafts
Time drafts
Documents against Payment (D/P)
Documents against Acceptance (A/P)
Open Account
Extended terms
Telegraphic (wire) transfer

Getting Better Payment Terms
Negotiate for successively better terms
Reduce order lead times
Pay with drafts instead of letters of credit
Issue L/Cs, drafts at usance
Open account, setoffs
Take delivery closer to destination

APPENDIX 6A: FORECASTING EXCHANGE RATE CHANGES

Exchange rate forecasting is a long-term exercise. Short-term forecasting of exchange rates has as many unknown variables as does the long-term but some of the variables begin to average out. Several studies have been done to see if general trends of exchange rates can be predicted with any degree of accuracy; the consensus is that they can.

Purchasing Power Parity

The case for forecasting exchange rates begins with the economic theory of purchasing power parity between two countries. Purchasing power parity means that the cost of similar or like items in two different countries will remain the same in both countries over the long term. If US$1:2.0DM and a loaf of bread costs $1 in the United States, a similar loaf of bread should cost 2.0 deutsche marks in West Germany. The mechanism by which this occurs over the long term happens as follows: Exchange rates between two countries will move in the op-posite way to the difference between the inflation rates (price changes) of the two countries. In other words, if the inflation rate of country A is 10 percent and country B is 6 percent, A's currency can be expected to devalue by the difference of 4 percent against B's currency. So the cost of a similar basket of goods in each country will remain relatively the same.

The logic behind this is somewhat involved but basically says that if A's prices, which rise 10 percent with its inflation, are not offset by a decrease in the exchange rate, A's goods will become overpriced in the international market. A loss in exports will create a trade deficit for A with resulting downward pressure on the exchange rate to com-pensate for A's weakening economic situation. This economic theory is well tested and works rather well over the long term. (Over the short term, other forces can intervene to temporarily counteract the effects noted above. These forces can include, for example, government in-tervention in foreign exchange markets to artificially peg exchange rates or time lags as the exchange markets react slowly to daily events.)

The Fisher Effect

The next step in the case for a long-term forecast of exchange rates involves a theory called the *Fisher Effect*, named for the economist who noted and did the first testing of the theory. Basically, Fisher postulated and showed that investors have a target rate of return that consists of two parts: a real rate of return and an additional rate of return to compensate for expected inflation. For example, if investors want 4 percent real return on their investment and inflation is expected to be 6 percent, these investors expect a total return of at least 10 percent on their investment. Interest rate returns for investments will have to be at least 10 percent to attract investors; interest rate returns of less than 10 percent will not attract investors. (Returns on some types of investments will have to be even higher than 10 percent if the in-vestment carries some additional risks, such as stocks.)

The Fisher Effect applies to exchange rates as follows: The differ-ence between the interest rates of two countries should be matched by an opposite movement of their exchange rates in the future contract market. For example, if A's interest rates are 10 percent and B's are 6 percent, A's currency would be expected to weaken 4 percent in relation to B's currency over time. The logic, simplified somewhat here, basi-cally says that investments are similar to the purchase of other goods even though investments are measured over time. Therefore investments carry much the same rationale for movement of exchange rates as with purchasing power parity.

Interest Rate Parity

The last step in the case for long-term forecasting of exchange rates involves the theory of interest rate parity between currencies. Interest rate parity says that the difference between interest received for similar investments of roughly equal risk and length of time in countries A and B will be offset by an opposite change in the forward contract rates for their respective currencies. The logic behind this follows similar reasoning to the Fisher Effect and purchasing power parity.

For example, if the interest rates for 90-day commercial paper is 10 percent in country A and 6 percent in country B, the 90-day forward contract rate should show a 4-percent devaluation in A's currency relative to B's currency.

See Stonehill and Eiteman for a clear and concise explanation of the above theories in their book *Finance: An International Perspective* (Homewood, Ill.: R. D. Irwin, 1987). For readers wishing to read the original source material see Irving Fisher, *The Purchasing Power of Money* (New York: Macmillan, 1911) or Irving Fisher, *Theory of Interest* (New York: Macmillan, 1930).

Making the Attempt to Forecast Exchange Rates

Those who want to try to forecast exchange rates will need to get data for inflation rates, interest rates, and exchange rates for the countries involved in the study. In addition, the following will also be needed:

- a computer with enough space to hold the data and perform some analysis;
- a *data base* software package to efficiently manipulate the data;
- statistical software to analyze the data; and
- graphics software to show the results of the study.

Information about current and future projections regarding inflation rates and interest rates for the vendor's country and the United States should be available from several sources. The vendor will be a source for this information, as will be the consulate of the vendor's country. Also, one or more of the major banks doing business internationally can be contacted; these banks employ specialists whose job it is to know information such as inflation rates. As a last resort, the

U.S. Department of Commerce can be contacted to get this information. Although the Department of Commerce is working to improve exports (not imports) of U.S. goods, it will have this information as part of the economic background it gives to companies that are trying to increase exports.

The simplest way to begin is to get data for only the countries where current vendors are located. The study can be enlarged at any time to include information about potential sourcing locations as well. First, all countries that peg their currencies to either another specific currency or a basket of currencies should be identified. If the currency is pegged to the U.S. dollar, there is no risk; if the currency is pegged to another foreign currency, data on this new currency will have to be gathered; if the currency is pegged to a basket of currencies, the exchange rate will (usually) change more conservatively, that is, with less risk.

The data to be gathered should cover a period of years in order to see long-term trends. Interest rate data from nearly all countries are available on at least a monthly basis. Inflation data will be available in highly developed countries on a monthly basis but from lesser-developed countries on a quarterly or even annual basis. The study should track the interest rate, the inflation rate, and the exchange rate, paying special attention to the differences between the rates as noted above.

The data should be entered in the data base. The sourcing executive may wish to get some help, if necessary, to learn how to enter the data and how to read the output of the statistical models, which can show how strong the correlations are between the data. The statistical package should have a time series analysis package to show the trend lines in the data. The graphics software should be able to show not only charts of the raw data but also the trend line information from the time series analysis. From the information received, an estimate of the direction of changes in exchange rates can be forecasted and the effect on the sourcing situation can be evaluated.

CHAPTER 7

MANAGING THE RELATIONSHIP FOR PEAK PERFORMANCE

A Fortune 500 company was supplying a major grocery chain's traffic-building promotion program. After a successful test market both the company and the grocery chain demanded additional product, both to capitalize on the popularity of the promotion and to forestall competing promotions. Existing suppliers were unable to produce any more than had originally been ordered but offered to make tools for any other source that might have capacity. A third source had recently been located but had not been qualified.

Prices and quantities were negotiated and an order placed over the telephone. The tools were sent and a letter of credit was issued payable upon shipment. All production was shipped direct to the customer's warehouse.

Less than 30 percent of the total shipment was of acceptable quality. The promotion schedule had to be completely revised and relations with the customer were severely strained. Faxes, telexes, and telephone calls to the supplier went unanswered and, when a visit was finally made, the factory was closed. The company wrote off 70 percent of the order, an amount in excess of $150,000.

A far less blatant example of supplier mismanagement almost cost a small electronics company its largest customer. The product used a unique integrated circuit, custom-made by a manufacturer that had the circuit assembled in the Philippines. Although the circuit had shown some evidence of intermittent failure, no effort was made to determine the reason for the problem, since it appeared in fewer than one-half of 1 percent of the circuits.

This seemingly insignificant failure rate, however, was appearing in an expensive product selling at a rate of 40,000 units per month and generating 200 irate customers every month.

Finally recognizing the urgency and severity of the problem, the small company, with the circuit manufacturer in tow, visited the assembly plant in the Philippines in a frantic attempt to repair the damage. Company representatives discovered that automatic equipment used to make a tiny connection in the circuit was out of calibration and, in fact, had never been calibrated. The faulty connections were never discovered because the part was being completely encapsulated in plastic immediately after the connection was made.

The equipment was calibrated and the assembler now tests two parts every hour to help ensure that it remains correctly calibrated.

Managing an offshore supplier is much the same as managing a domestic one. Except for the time differences. . . . And the language barriers and the cost of communication and especially the cost of making a visit when something goes wrong. Failures to communicate result in the same problems, and they cost even more to fix. Errors take longer to surface and longer to correct. Negotiating price adjustments and implementing cost reductions take longer because of language problems and the delays imposed by different time zones. In short, to achieve the same results, managing an offshore supplier takes much more time and effort.

Unfortunately, the very competitive pricing that is often achievable offshore will rarely compensate for even "acceptable" delivery and quality. All of the factors that complicate buying offshore tend to magnify the impact of even the smallest mistakes. Fortunately, there is an effective means of managing suppliers that minimizes the impact of mistakes and eliminates most unwelcome surprises.

MANAGING DELIVERY PERFORMANCE

Effective supplier delivery performance requires taking steps early in a relationship to prevent late deliveries, rather than various reactions to a delivery that is already late. A very effective delivery program can be broken into five steps:

1. Set delivery performance objectives with the supplier.
2. Measure delivery performance.

3. Set up an early warning system.

4. Hold regular performance reviews.

5. Reward good performance.

This rather simple process is certainly not limited to buying offshore but it provides a good model with which to discuss some peculiar elements of managing deliveries from an offshore supplier.

Set Delivery Performance Objectives with the Supplier

Mundane as it may seem, this may prove to be the most difficult element of the delivery management system. Almost invariably, a supplier's approach to good delivery performance will be to ask for earlier orders, to prohibit the rescheduling of orders, and to restrict changes to the product. In contrast, buyers demand quick reaction to new orders and a highly flexible response to changes.

The performance objectives must be a carefully negotiated set of commitments between buyer and seller: how early orders must be placed, how rapidly orders may be increased, how changes must be handled and who will pay for them, how exceptions will be treated, and so on. All of these conditions might be agreed upon easily with a domestic supplier but are of much greater significance offshore because of the greater costs of failure.

Buying offshore adds a degree of complexity to stating the objectives. Delivery may be made well before the buyer sees the shipment; late arrival at the buyer's dock may not reflect poor supplier performance. Receipt of a letter of credit may trigger the start of production; bank transmission delays should be the responsibility of the buyer. The many differences in national holidays will require considerable cooperation and communication; Japan virtually shuts down for Golden Week, most of Chinese-speaking Asia shuts down for (Chinese) New Year, and much of Europe is gone for the month of August, as is the United States for Christmas.

Buying offshore also sharpens awareness of the need for some fairly precise objectives. Merely extending order lead times is hardly an adequate solution for a cash-poor supplier; it simply increases the investment in inventory. Moreover, since buying offshore will increase shipping time, few buyers are willing to extend order times as well.

The objectives should be explicit but simple and measurable: explicit so both supplier and buyer know precisely what is expected; simple to facilitate intercultural or interlingual communication; and measurable so they can be used effectively.

- "All deliveries as initially stated in the letters of credit; none renegotiated for shipment delays."
- "All deliveries received by buyer's forwarder on or before due date but no more than five days before due date."
- "Applies to all orders placed 90 or more days before due date. Other orders will be accepted on a best-effort basis."

Measure and Report Delivery Performance

To be effective, performance measurement must be visible, serious, consistent, and promptly reported.

As the now-famous case study of a production line being observed for the effects of music upon performance demonstrated, the mere knowledge that something is being measured, or even observed, will improve performance. In the case of the production line, of course, production improved whether or not music was being played, and independent of its type or speed, merely because the production workers knew they were being observed. Merely taking a measurement, then, will not achieve the same results as taking and reporting it to the organization being measured. As a corollary to this, it should be obvious that judicious dissemination of the measurement will be more effective than burying it in a quarterly summary. If the salesperson handling an account and the plant manager producing the product are each aware the other is receiving a delivery performance report, both will work to ensure they do not provide causes for delay.

Reporting must be taken seriously by the buyer's organization. Lax, indifferent reporting, inaccurate reports, even sloppily prepared reports will tend to diminish any response they may elicit. If prompt and accurate delivery is to be perceived by the supplier as a serious issue to the buyer, the buyer's measurement and reporting must reinforce that perception. Every delivery must be recorded, not merely the exceptions, to focus on good performance. The seriousness of any exceptions can be reinforced by elevating the report distribution—the plant manager sees every delivery report, the general manager is notified of late shipments.

The measurement and reporting must be consistent. By taking the measurement and reporting it the same way each time, a standard of performance can be established against which exceptions or the need for improvement can be compared. Consistent reporting also lends itself to establishing targets. Measuring the shipments differently—some to a forwarder's receipt, some to customs clearance, some to delivery—will obscure any common elements that might be used to define improvement.

Prompt reporting accomplishes two things: It substantiates the seriousness the buyer attributes to delivery performance, and it provides quick feedback of problems to the supplier. The identification of problems is facilitated by promptness; errors or situations that contributed to delay will be more easily remembered if complaint of a late delivery follows quickly upon its arrival.

Set up an Early Warning System

Many companies do not discover that a shipment is late until its due date has passed. Many do not even learn that a shipment was late until the material is needed, often days or weeks after the due date. Some companies are so uncertain of their deliveries that they are *pleased* when a supplier notifies them that a shipment will be late.

None of this is necessary. All the information necessary to monitor the progress of an order is available somewhere within the supplier's organization and very little is needed to make use of it. As an example, consider the monitoring that normally accompanies the introduction of a new product: "Do you have all the material yet?"; "Have you sent the parts to production yet?"; "Did everything pass?"; "Have you shipped it yet?"

An early warning system institutionalizes such monitoring

and can be as simple or complex as need requires. Implementing the system can be part of pilot production and should start with the first order. The system relies largely on collecting and communicating information that is already being produced and used by the supplier and making further use of it to inform the buyer that progress is being made on an order.

Milestones in an Early Warning System

Dated, formal acknowledgment of an order.   At a minimum, and whether or not any other attempt is made to implement this program, demand order acknowledgments. Myriad problems could cause an order to be missed or delayed when buying offshore. A prompt acknowledgment is probably the simplest and least-expensive method of assuring timely delivery.

Special Materials.   Tooling orders, in particular, may require special materials, but any product that incorporates expensive, unusual, or difficult-to-obtain material can be subject to confirmation: "Please acknowledge by (date) that the material needed for this product has been ordered and promised for delivery on a schedule consistent with the requirements of this Purchase Order." The lack of such acknowledgment might prompt a buyer to other courses of action, or assistance in seeking the material.

Materials Staging.   Assembling various materials needed for production is virtually indistinguishable from releasing it to production in many large, continuous process industries. Elsewhere, especially in developing industries offshore, staging material is a distinct and important step in production. The status of kit staging might be particularly important, for example, if an insufficient amount of only one commodity were available for a production order while the letter of credit issued for the product prohibited partial shipments. Would the buyer be interested in such information?

Release to Production.   Almost without exception, a manufacturer can state with a high degree of certainty exactly how long it will take to produce a product once all the raw materials are available. An on-time release to production, therefore, is an almost certain guarantee that an order will ship on time. And it is an almost certain guarantee that a late release won't ship on time or, and possibly worse, that production will be rushed to meet the delivery schedule.

Inspection results.   If the ultimate "Oops" is selling bad product to your customer and a major "Oops" is receiving bad product from your supplier, notification that a production run was bad, before additional shipping and duty costs and the loss of time to find the problem, has to be at worst a minor "oops." Problems happen, and it is better to find that out early, rather than after a shipment has been at sea for a month, the duties paid, and no time is left to recover from the error.

Shipping notification.   It's on its way! How many shipped? To many buyers there remains a window of opportunity to manage receipt of the order. If the supplier has been instructed to make delivery to the buyer's forwarder, the buyer can still manage the mode of transportation: Ship 500 by air (at $1.00 apiece) for a customer willing to pay for an accelerated delivery and the rest by sea (at a dime apiece).

For some products it may not be necessary to receive any of this reporting, although failing to demand order acknowledgment is probably foolish. For other products the list may be far from adequate to provide acceptable assurance of timely delivery. In either case, the information should become a regular part of the relationship between buyer and seller. All of the information is regularly prepared by the supplier. Even if the data is in another language there is no need for regular translation; if it is always reported the same way, just translate the form once and fill in the blanks. What is important is that an agreement is reached to provide the data for each order and that an immediate, and forceful, complaint is raised every time the data fail to appear.

Hold Regular Performance Reviews

Performance reviews serve some important purposes: They reaffirm the importance of good delivery performance; they provide a strong reminder that measurements are made of delivery performance; and they provide a high-level forum in which to seek corrective action.

Simply scheduling a review will precipitate an intensive evaluation of performance by the supplier. Preparation for a review will normally result in a flurry of internal reviews as successive layers of the supplier's organization prepare for a meeting with the buyer. If measurement has been extensive and widely reported, the supplier will prepare to address any problems that may have been encountered or, if performance has been good, will identify and reaffirm the procedures that seem to work.

Lack of agreed on objectives, good measurement, or regular reporting may open the proceedings to disagreement and recrimination. A supplier can hardly be held accountable for performance standards with which it had not agreed, or for failure to correct problems of which it was never informed.

At best, a performance review will include members of both the supplier and buyer's companies who are familiar with the operations affecting deliveries and managers empowered to correct problems.

Reward Good Performance

Even the best companies treasure and display awards and affidavits that affirm their excellence. This is especially true offshore, where suppliers are more often competing for international business. Simple thanks for good performance is so inexpensive, yet so valuable to both supplier and buyer, that they should be a regular extension of supplier management.

First, to the supplier, gestures of appreciation are of real value. Foyers displaying plaques and certificates acknowledging superior performance, or awards for superior delivery or quality, affirm the supplier's successful participation in the international business community. They provide an unsolicited recommendation to whoever visits.

The company making the award will accrue several benefits. The award will serve as a constant reminder that it is a customer, and one that is sufficiently concerned about supplier performance to recognize and reward it when well done. Having received an award, most suppliers will strive to equal or better their performances during the next measurement period; they know they are being measured and by what standards.

Making such awards should become a regular part of supplier management. To ensure that it happens, plan periodic internal reviews with the intent of identifying suppliers eligible for such attention and make sure that at least some minimum number receive attention. The possibilities for rewards are nearly endless: supplier of the year or month, best delivery record, highest quality for the period, zero defects for the period, most improved.

MONITORING QUALITY PERFORMANCE

For those familiar with the techniques, the foregoing discussion of delivery management may appear to be a simplistic analogue of the process management approaches espoused by Deming, Crosby, Taguchi, or several others. With apologies to all of them, it might be, although the practice of calling up a supplier to see if an order would ship on time probably preceded any of them.

Compared to quality management, ensuring consistent delivery is relatively simple. Nevertheless, the underlying approach of identifying problems early in the process is the same whether it is delivery or quality that is being managed. To the extent to which this similarity in approach does exist, then, the delivery performance model can serve as a basis for discussion of quality management. However, the multitudinous requirements of quality management—the complexity involved in establishing standard for performance, of taking and reporting measurements, and of analyzing and responding to discrepancies—permit only an overview of it here but one that will, we hope, serve as an adequate guide to understanding the process.

Waiting for orders to arrive before inspecting them is a risky and expensive approach to supplier management. Discovering defects just when a product is needed is more than exasperating, it is expensive. If the product is the result of many weeks work, such shipments result in one of several reactions, all of them undesirable:

- Reject and return the shipment for rework or replacement.
- Maintain a safety stock, that is, keep enough parts on hand to satisfy requirements until the shipment is replaced.
- Rework the parts before using them.
- Use the parts anyway.

Each undesirable solution generally further exacerbates the problem. Round-trip shipping costs, often by air, are added to the cost for returns. Duty may have to be paid again upon the product's return. Safety stock inventories must be increased to account for increased shipping time and customs clearance. Who pays for the rework will become a matter of dispute until the supplier gets a sample to confirm the discrepancy. The tendency to use "marginal" product increases.

Extrapolating from the early warning approach to delivery management, quality assurance management focuses on monitoring the production process at each critical step to detect errors and, then, correcting them before the process continues. To be effective, the system greatly expands upon the few points at which delivery schedules can be monitored.

FIVE BASIC STEPS TO MONITOR QUALITY

1. Understand and specify what are to be the acceptable limits of variation in each area of the product specification for it to meet minimum requirements—measurements, materials, finish, color, whatever.

2. Quantify the standards and measure the results of production continually, recording each measurement for comparison against the standard.

3. Understand how each part of the manufacturing process must perform to ensure that each standard is maintained. Establish minimum standards for each operation in the production process.

4. Confirm that the process is repeatable; that every time an operation is performed its result meets the expected standards. Document the process and ensure that it will

not be changed without ensuring that any changes will also meet standards.

5. Review the measurements against the established standards and continue or correct the process as necessary to maintain acceptable performance.

At the extremes of process management—controlling nuclear power generation or in continuous manufacturing processes, for example—measurement and feedback control take place in seconds, or milliseconds. Dozens of operations may be monitored at the instant each occurs, and results are transmitted to controls that respond immediately, including controls that will shut down the process. Discrete processes can be structured for such control as well. The most sophisticated process control systems, for both continuous and discrete manufacturing, use computers to automatically measure, analyze, and provide feedback.

Just as in the case of delivery management, however, process need only be as simple or complex as the requirement, or the cost of mistakes, require. If the process is slow enough and the cost of inventory low enough, each part could be inspected after each operation. More likely, a sampling method will be used, which might range from simple to complex, from "two samples every hour" to sample sizes determined by MIL Standard AQL tables. The effects are the same: a periodic snapshot confirming the process' ability to produce parts that meet specifications.

Many manufacturers monitor their processes regularly, or may have fully implemented Statistical Process Control (SPC), independent of any urging to do so by their customers. The reason is simple; the earlier an error is discovered the fewer faulty parts will be produced. This translates into less scrap and, ultimately, fewer rejected shipments and fewer reruns. To the off-shore supplier, it also avoids incurring double freight costs, or airfreight replacement of rejected material as well.

Even if a supplier is not monitoring its production process well, a buyer can request that measurements of at least an early warning nature begin. This is especially true if faulty shipments have already been made; asking the supplier to determine whether work still in process at its plant are similarly faulty may save both buyer and seller time and money. Both supplier and buyer might agree that several, specific parameters will be fairly representative of the overall quality of the product, parameters relating to plating thickness or surface finish on tableware, for example. Samples taken from each lot could be inspected to ensure that a critical process is still within tolerance. Even destructive testing will readily be justified. Consider in the plating example what the impact of having *twice* as much silver as necessary on a spoon would mean to the supplier.

The process of precious metals plating is one that will already be monitored carefully, the feedback used to ensure that plating thickness *never* significantly exceeds the minimum. Very often, it may also regularly permit the process to fall below the minimum, especially if the customer is inattentive. Although the costs of not having enough silver may not approach having twice as much as needed, if a buyer ensures that every shipment with deficient plating is returned, the process will be monitored for both the minimum and the maximum. The cost of having thousands of spoons returned for not having enough silver will warrant the additional attention.

SUPPLIER QUALITY MEASUREMENT AND REPORTING

The buyer's objective will be to ensure that a supplier is practicing process management. The original plant survey should indicate whether a supplier is practicing statistical process control (SPC) or has sufficient monitors of its process in place to reasonably ensure consistent quality. The next step is to ensure that each of the buyer's shipments receive the benefit of the system. If no such system is in place, the objective will be to agree on such monitors as are required and ensure the agreement is implemented.

Confirming compliance is simple: Ask for the data. If the system is established to provide early warning of problems, have in-process inspection results sent at the time they are made. If sufficient lot and order number information is provided, the data will both confirm that the shipment is being produced on time and, to that point in the process, meets specifications.

If several in-process monitors are being used, require that

any final inspection reconfirm the measurements reported for each, in effect verifying the process of measurement itself. Require that each shipment include the final inspection samples for that shipment, as well as the measurements made of those samples. If a number of suppliers are involved in the process, require each to submit their in-process and final inspection reports to both the buyer and the next supplier.

REVIEW THE MEASUREMENTS, CORRECT THE PROBLEMS

The most effective use of process management is to identify and eliminate the causes of error in the production system. Merely identifying a discrepancy or noting that the process is not producing to specification ignores the basic intent of process management, to identify the cause of the discrepancy so it can be eliminated. The system is not failing if the supplier reports a discrepancy; it is failing if the supplier fails to correct the cause of the discrepancy. Measurements showing out-of-tolerance parts, accompanied by a report that production was stopped and the cause corrected, is a demonstration of success, not failure. Failure would be shipping the bad parts, or not fixing the problem.

Measurement and reporting is not control of the process, it is an attempt to confirm that a supplier has its process under management. If the reports aren't used or if frivolous or irrelevant use is made of the data, little benefit will be derived from the system. Prompt recognition and responsive use of the system will gradually improve the system.

When errors are discovered, correcting the problem implies determining the cause and eliminating it. Solutions that obscure the cause, or appear to have eliminated a problem without actually determining what caused it, are not meaningful solutions. The supplier's objective in using a process management system should be to identify and eliminate the cause, thereby avoiding any future recurrence or expense.

Recognize that such a system will probably be in a continual state of change, or improvement, as flaws in the process are detected or discrepancies in the product reveal deficiencies in the monitoring process. Some parts of the process may come under such tight control that measurement may be relaxed, others may require more frequent observation. Ultimately, both supplier and buyer may place enough confidence in the management and measurement of the process that incoming material is no longer inspected. Dock-to-stock qualification of a supplier implies that its shipments go directly into stock, Just-in-time (JIT) shipments never go to stock, but go immediately to the production line. Neither disposition of a shipment is possible without a complete implementation of a process management system, but even a few early warning monitors can improve the quality of, and permit visibility into, a supplier's process.

PRICE MANAGEMENT AND COST CONTAINMENT

A buyer's responses to price increases are the same with domestic as with offshore suppliers: competitive pressure, encouraging greater efficiency, finding ways to reduce cost, and so forth. Nevertheless, the greater complexity of buying offshore adds new variables to the problem. Although any given scenario will require action uniquely appropriate to it, following are examples of a few situations not encountered domestically. In each of them, the buyer who is intimately familiar with both the process of making and delivering a product and of its individual cost components will be best able to defend against a price increase.

Exchange rates are a frequent, and frequently abused, excuse for a price increase. As often as not, however, the offending exchange rate only partially affects cost or is offset by other changes. Low labor rates, not material cost, are often the reason for buying from any given offshore supplier. Any material used is often available at prices fairly constant worldwide, and, moreover, traded in U.S. dollars, meaning that local exchange rate changes should have little or no effect on material or, consequently, product cost. In fact, if the local currency appreciates against the dollar, the supplier's costs may actually fall, not increase.

Similarly, price increases blamed wholly on material costs

are as difficult to justify as those based wholly on exchange rates. At issue again is how much of the product cost is reflected in its material content and how much of that can be denominated in U.S. dollars. Even when the increase in the cost of materials is substantial, except in respect of a few unique or precious materials, less-expensive alternate materials or sources may be available to offset rising local costs.

Exchange rates are also, partially, a reflection of efficiency, of productivity. An exchange rate may appear to have had an unfavorable impact on cost but may also have been more than offset by reductions in the labor content of the product. Quotations generally reflect a supplier's expected cost to produce the quantities requested on the first order. The experience gained during the initial production usually reduces the labor required for subsequent orders. Sure, labor rates may increase over time, but if labor content has been correspondingly reduced, any pressure to increase price can't be substantiated by the need to recover increased costs of labor.

Offshore suppliers do suffer more than their domestic counterparts from their customers' lack of planning and foresight and, quite justifiably, often demand compensation for the lack. At issue often is the buyer's insensitivity to the costs of expediting for an offshore manufacturer. Components or materials readily available in the United States albeit at a premium, are frequently imported when needed elsewhere. Singapore, for example, although a major worldwide supplier of electronic assemblies, produces few integrated circuits. At the same time, few distributors carry inventories adequate to the requirements of most orders, emergency stocks perhaps, but not on-site inventories equivalent to those of U.S. electronics distributors. Most quotations reflect the cost of imported components, at both the supplier's standard lead times and at the least-cost mode of transportation. Orders placed with short lead times, therefore, add more than the cost of a little overtime—they may substantially increase the cost of materials.

Short-notice changes, too, will wreak havoc with an offshore supplier's costs. Quotations usually assume that needed materials can be ordered immediately after the customer's order is accepted. Replacing any of this material, in reaction to customer change orders, implies canceling some orders and ordering something else. This is likely to result in cancellation charges for the first order and some penalty in price or service for the replacement order. Although such service may be a common expectation when ordering from a domestic supplier, the costs that accrue to an offshore supplier will frequently be billed to the customer.

Few offshore suppliers will not long be forgiving of orders placed with insufficient lead times or of change orders made without adequate notice. If a buyer is not in a position to correct, compensate for, or otherwise overcome the lack of planning and foresight that leads to such practices, buying offshore will probably not result in any significant savings.

STAY ON TOP OF THE RELATIONSHIP

The promise of perfect systems notwithstanding, every buyer knows that sometimes even the best-planned order will go astray. Buying offshore offers no insurance against occurrences of this sort and will, of course, entail even greater obstacles to getting things sorted out: Time differences make scheduling telephone calls a nuisance, various national and religious holidays always seem to coincide with a production problem, and communications have a way of breaking down at the height of a crisis.

Troubleshooting an offshore supplier will benefit from some groundwork laid independent of the formal systems of management, particularly if good personal relations can be developed at a number of levels within both companies. Develop a number of contacts within the supplier's organization. Don't depend on a single channel. A buyer's sole contact will invariably be on vacation or on a business trip when an emergency arises. In addition, ensure that several levels of both companies are in regular contact. Trade home telephone numbers with the principal contacts within a supplier's organization; a couple of days of missed messages during a crisis will quickly justify the precaution.

Take a more formal approach to addressing problems. The very often casual approach to business within the United States tends to obscure the strong impression a strict and formal complaint may have internationally. This is especially true across a language barrier. A succinct description of a problem and strong request for its correction may be all that is necessary for its correction. The leverage of purchase orders and letters of credit can also be applied to the same end. If particular problems seem to persist, address them specifically when issuing an order or, if they are being used, in any letters of credit.

Keep detailed records of communications. Because communication will usually be limited to snippets of text over the fax machine, or brief, expensive telephone calls, plan regular, periodic visits to stay abreast of growth and changes. Verify the implementation of any of the myriad conditions or responsibilities imposed on the supplier: specific agreements in process implementation, the maintenance of safety stocks, or the condition of tools. Review with the supplier developments in both companies: financial condition, new customers, new business, any particulars that might change the nature of the relationship.

THE ULTIMATE SOLUTION: TERMINATING THE RELATIONSHIP

The signs of many unacceptable relationships are the same whether domestic or offshore: Real support by the buyer is rewarded by erratic delivery and quality; "fixes" are implemented for show but not in reality; attempts are made to renegotiate specifications every time they are not met; agreed on corrections are ignored; and/or there are frequent and unjustified increases in price. Tables 7.1 and 7.2 illustrate positive and negative signs in offshore relationships.

In addition, buying from one country or company offshore may give rise to a number of other situations that can only be addressed by buying elsewhere. Exchange rates may, indeed, drive prices beyond profitable levels; the increased value of the yen has forced all but fully automated production, and expensive traditional handcraft, to other countries. Some economies have deteriorated so badly that the communication and transportation infrastructure needed to do business is so weakened that pur-

TABLE 7-1
Positive Signs of a Working Partnership

The supplier takes responsibility for solutions to problems:

Alerts customer to impending problems and suggests appropriate
    corrections.
Accepts reject returns and is responsive to replacement.
Corrects problems in scheduling and quality control.
Takes an active role in cost reduction.
Initiates new or backup tooling as required for regular production.
Initiates improvements in design, process, and/or product technology to
    meet changing competitive conditions.
Responds quickly to queries and suggested ideas for action.

Reasonable responses by the supplier to problems and errors:

Warns of impending changes in lead times.
Points out overspecifications, design flaws, and other problems in
    customer documents before wasting time on them.
Knows customer order patterns and may place orders for raw materials
    and/or subcontracted parts without customer's confirmed order.
Will reschedule (within reason) with no penalty to customer.
Willingly reassigns material from canceled orders to other jobs and
    customers, or will try to resell or return to reduce cost impact of
    cancelled orders.

---

chasing is impaired. No one would have predicted that Tancredo
Neves, newly elected president of Brazil, would die before taking
office in 1985. But even before Neves died, observers were already noting that Sarney, Neves's vice-president, appeared to
be weak and possibly unable to implement the policies that were
required to bring order to Brazil's economic chaos. Brazil's loss
of Neves cost it uncounted orders as its economy continued to
falter.

Political changes often force a separation. China's significant
international sales plummeted after its problems at Tiananmen
Square and, particularly, its government's reaction to the outrage
expressed by the rest of the world. Sri Lanka appeared to be
close in line to follow Singapore, Hong Kong, and Taiwan as
another Asian "wonder" until the Tamil insurgency interfered.

Then too, the buyer and supplier simply grow apart, either
into increasingly different lines of endeavor, or by one outgrow-
ing the other, two situations that occur far more frequently be-

TABLE 7–2
Profile of a Buyer's Nightmare

Poor Order Management

The supplier constantly needs to have orders confirmed and reconfirmed.
The supplier never knows order status at periodic meetings ("I'll check" is the regular response).
The supplier's organization does not communicate with itself; sales accepts orders but does not tell production, production does not order raw material, etc.
Safety stock is paid for but does not exist.
Capacity not reserved for orders with adequate lead time.
Cancellation charges approach product costs and the supplier will not discuss a more appropriate response.
Delivery schedules are met sporadically, not consistently.

Marginal Quality

Quality "fixes" are implemented for show, not in fact.
Root causes of quality defects are uncovered and eliminated.
Agreed on procedures are ignored.
The supplier tries to renegotiate specifications every time they are not met.
Argument, delay, or recrimination accompanies valid rejects.
Product specifications are consistently missed.

Price

Price increases are arbitrary, not tied to cost increases.
Competition for labor increases but there is no attempt to control and/or reduce labor content.
When one cost element is reduced, another always goes up.
Unreasonable demands are made for more volume to "maintain" price.
There are too many miniscule price reductions after major cost reductions.
Specification changes result in arbitrary price increases not related to cost.
Prices of new products far exceed prices of old, similar products.

tween international firms than between domestic neighbors. In any of these cases, disengaging from a supplier presents issues that, if not unique, are at least exacerbated when the supplier is offshore. The following suggestions may never become necessary—few separations are actually hostile—but do reflect some normal precautions.

ISSUES TO CONSIDER WHEN BREAKING AN OFFSHORE SUPPLIER RELATIONSHIP

- The supplier community may be a goldfish bowl.
- Copyright and other legal protection may be weak.
- Tools and material will be difficult to recover.

The Supplier Community May Be a Goldfish Bowl

Within a given country, member companies of the same industry are often in close communication. Industry associations may be far stronger than in the United States and under none of the restraints imposed by U.S. trade laws. What would be considered collusion in the United States is often legal—apportioning business to available capacity, for example. In some places, businesses of the same type are traditionally in the same family or group of families or highly concentrated in the same region.

The implication of breaking a relationship with an offshore supplier will be obvious; it may not be possible to replace a supplier in the same country without announcing an intended separation with the first supplier. Doing so is not impossible, of course, but may require more tact than would be necessary to do the same thing in the United States. Timing such a move during the transition to a new product or process, or during a period of exceptional demand would, at least, offer some plausible excuse for initial purchases from the new supplier.

Copyright and Other Legal Protection May Be Weak

Any move, and especially one that may not be wholly amicable, should be planned well in advance. Arrange, perhaps, for drawings to be purged for revision or correction to ensure that as many sensitive drawings or documents as possible can be recovered prior to the final break. Update any nondisclosure agreements if they have not been kept current. Although every attempt should be made to manage the break to avoid litigation, having current written assurances of confidentiality may preclude the need for action later.

Clean up open order reports to ensure that material is not

being ordered against unneeded requirements or the result of sloppy order management. Verify that any orders filled "short" are formally closed. Verify that payables are managed to ensure last-shipment quality and completeness, or to provide leverage for the recovery of documents, tools, or material. A hefty payable would prove a far better inducement to performance than hollow threats of legal action.

Tools and Material Will Be More Difficult to Recover

Mere distance would complicate these issues even if there were no extenuating circumstances. Nevertheless, do not assume that moving a production tool will ever be easy. It may be, but it is equally likely that its disposition will require some careful planning.

Certainly, no supplier will relinquish a tool until any and all outstanding invoices, discrepant material claims, and other unfinished business have been concluded to the supplier's satisfaction. In addition, the tools or materials are in the supplier's jurisdiction and legal action anywhere outside the United States is highly unlikely to be productive.

Even under the most cordial separations, additional care should be exercised. Tools or material may be allowed to deteriorate between the initial request for return and the actual pickup or shipment. A molding tool, for example, that was inadequately prepared for storage after use may be worthless.

Under less than cordial circumstances the tools may be "difficult to find" or even sabotaged. As an added precaution, once the decision has been made to pull out of a supplier, arrange for the tool to be inspected or, even better, pulled for "modification." Both tool deterioration owing to poor management and deliberate sabotage have occurred and will continue to occur, although few suppliers are willing to risk their reputation by permitting or admitting either. Planning and tact are important, however, if there is any possibility that moving a tool will be troublesome, and anything is possible if a relationship is being broken in anger.

MANAGING A TOOL FOR MOVEMENT

- Inspect tools regularly, both to stay apprised of their condition and to know their location. This is not easy when the supplier is in the crowded conditions of Hong Kong or Taiwan, for example, but persistence will pay dividends.
- Develop a separate relationship with the toolmaking firm, if it is a different company from the supplier. It is relatively easy to have a tool returned for "repairs" or "modification" and then to pick it up at the toolmaker's location. Here, though, the goldfish bowl situation may hamper some of these plans.
- Manage payables to the supplier to ensure that the outstanding payable is worth more than the tool in question.
- Bring witnesses to "help with the move" to the pickup site, especially ones who may have a business relationship with the supplier other than the purchase in question.

SUMMARY

Control of an offshore supplier requires more constant attention than control of a domestic supplier if only because problems have far greater repercussions. Reactive management is a wholly inadequate approach; the pipeline of an offshore purchase is too long. If production defects are not discovered until the goods are inspected in the United States, the remedies are expensive and time consuming. Failures in communicating order increases or decreases both imply additional expense, either to expedite production and delivery or to hold excess inventory. Whether the additional expense is borne by the buyer or supplier is almost irrelevant in a long-term relationship; the buyer will ultimately bear the expense.

The best forms of control require suppliers to report the status of procurement and production as each step occurs, or to report exceptions that may occur at each step. Prompt notice of a problem usually allows time for an appropriate response, or a less-expensive response than later notice would allow. Both the order and production processes can be analyzed to determine which of their steps will best lend themselves to a supplier-reporting system.

CHECKLIST

Managing Delivery Performance
　　Set objectives
　　Measure and report performance
　　Set up an early warning system
　　Hold performance reviews
　　Reward good performance

Managing Quality Performance
　　Specify the requirements
　　Quantify the standards of performance
　　Ensure the production process results in a product that meets
　　　the specifications
　　Ensure the process is repeatable
　　Measure the results of production
　　Follow up on discrepancies

Offshore Cost Containment
　　Isolate exchange rate impacts
　　Improving efficiency
　　Impacts of buyer planning
　　Confirmations and verification

Terminating an Unworkable Relationship
　　Review the signs of a working partnership
　　Watch for the elements of a buyer's nightmare

Issues of terminating an offshore supplier
　　The goldfish bowl
　　Copyright and other legal protection
　　Recovering tools and material

AFTERWORD

Terminating an offshore supplier should force a reevaluation of the buyer's strategy, including the very decision to go offshore. How many of the problems that led to the dissolution were actually faults of the buyer or were inherent in the offshore relationship? Should the business have gone overseas at all?

Chapter 1 delineated some of the attributes of a promising offshore location: political stability, a strong infrastructure, and a well-educated urban workforce. The United States offers all of these and more. After the impact of the 1980s is assessed, the United States may rank among the best places to buy. Three processes already underway will promote this situation: a massive reduction of the U.S. military, the absorption of the USSR and the Eastern European economies into the world's economic mainstream, and the coalescence of three superregional economies. The first two of these will tend to *restrict* U.S. wage growth, forcing it to become more competitive; the latter will bring the United States some advantages in regional trade.

DEMILITARIZATION OF THE U.S. ECONOMY

Shortly before the 1990 war with Iraq, Secretary of Defense William Cheney stated that defense spending will be cut to the lowest level since before World War II over the next five years. Several hundred thousand servicepeople will ultimately leave the U.S. Armed Forces as a result of conventional force cutbacks in Europe. Those most likely to be retained have years of training and experience; those targeted for reduction are those near retirement and young, relatively inexperienced personnel. As in a private sector reduction in force, the poor performers will be the first to go. They will enter the work force with little applicable civilian training or experience.

In addition to reductions in military personnel, defense cutbacks will result in the elimination of a large number of civilian jobs. Numerous military bases have already been identified for closure, many of which provide employment for large civilian populations in their vicinities. The defense industries will lose jobs as programs are dropped or deliveries pushed out. In all, the American Electronics Association estimated that across all sectors of the economy, for each $1 billion cut from defense, 38,000 jobs will be lost. The war with Iraq merely delayed the reduction in military spending; neither the base closure process nor arms reductions negotiations with the USSR were affected. The impact will be to increase unemployment or, at best, retard real reductions in the unemployment rates. Either will depress wage growth.

The United States may not be expected to act as global police in the future, but no other country will replace its arms economy. The jobs that massive defense spending supported are not moving offshore; they are gone. Moreover, there is little reason to believe that the process of U.S. demilitarization will be reversed during the decade or that any of the other major industrial nations will become inclined to increase its armament. The constitutions of both Germany and Japan contain the legacy of World War II: They are "peace" constitutions and restrict both country's military forces. This is very unlikely to change. Neither could justify building its forces in the current environment of East-West cooperation and many other nations still fear the idea of either regaining military dominance. Neither had any significant military contribution in the war with Iraq. They both contributed money and that was quite enough as far as the rest of the world was concerned. The USSR is least likely to restart the arms race; that is exactly what led to its current predicament.

REBUILDING THE ECONOMIES OF THE USSR
AND EASTERN EUROPE

Globally, the economic pressures of the 1990s will stem principally from the massive task of assimilating the economies of the USSR and Eastern Europe into the economic mainstream. Far from being either simple or quick, this task will probably prove to be so complex, and the objectives of the participants so varied, that only in the retrospectives of future decades will the process be completely understood. Nevertheless, it should be possible to identify enough of the problems and pressures that will characterize the reform to help buyers discern where some of the most likely procurement opportunities will arise.

The process of assimilation will undoubtedly reflect both the historical relationships of the participants, and the means and goals of the countries that will fund the reform. The process will also undergo change as the strength of new alliances threatens old relationships. The historical relationships are the easiest to recognize: ancient antagonisms, fear of regained military dominance, reunited countries. Evidence abounds to help predict how several countries will approach the task: Japan with economic aid calculated to provide a long-term economic advantage; Germany by restoring itself as the focus of Europe; the United States attempting to maintain strategic balance everywhere. The impact of new relationships will be the hardest to predict. Will the USSR replace the United States as the world's supplier of many raw materials, or will it cooperate in controlling the steppes and the great plains, the world's breadbaskets?

Despite their lack of any significant armament, both Germany and Japan are so powerful economically and politically that many other countries' role in the reconstruction will include attempts to contain or counterbalance them by building the economic strength of others. The USSR, in particular, will receive considerable attention and support because no other economy is of sufficient size and proximity to provide such a counterbalance. Furthermore, support will be forthcoming from France and England as well as the United States, both of the former vitally interested in maintaining strategic balances with Germany.

Japan has an equal interest in ensuring the USSR has a vigorous economy, not to counterbalance Germany, but China.

President Nixon's historic visit was to draw China into the world economy and begin to develop it as a strategic balance to the USSR. China is now the ninth largest exporter to the United States and is rapidly becoming a threat to Japan's preeminence in Asia. The USSR is a major customer of India and the Asian countries. Their growth and Japan's position both depend on a strong Soviet economy.

Japan is also eager to gain access to the tremendous natural resources in western Siberia, particularly as they are both closer and potentially less expensive than other sources. Although considerable improvement in the Siberian infrastructure will be needed to obtain the resources at reasonable cost, with its tremendous wealth and strong political and economic motives to do so, Japan may be expected to make major investments and provide significant aid for their development. The funding may be massive, especially if it is in the form of industrial development loans, a form of aid that Japan has used to its benefit elsewhere for many years. Such loans are made to fund the development and export of a commodity. Japan then imports the commodity at the lowest possible prices as well as recovering the proceeds of the loan. Although Japan has been criticized for this apparently cynical form of aid, it may be the only way the USSR will receive all the financing it needs for the region.

In the 1990s, the reconstruction of the USSR's economy will probably not mean greater access to the products of Siberian resource development because only a few such programs will have much effect this decade, although some increased competition for the U.S. lumber industry will be evident sooner. It will also mean more global competition for high-labor-content products as previously communist economies begin to compete for business. For the United States, it will either mean that low-labor-content jobs will move offshore to these countries, or that wage increases for these jobs will continue to be very slow.

THE SUPERREGIONAL ECONOMIES

The inclusion of the USSR and the Eastern European nations into the world's economic mainstream will probably prompt the acceleration of several other processes already underway, notably the development of a regional economic community within the Western Hemisphere, and may spur the development of other regional alliances in reaction to it and the EEC. The United States will certainly be the focal provider of high-technology products in the Western Hemisphere, followed by Canada and the growing industrial economies in Central and South America.

The EEC has already been highly successful in attracting companies outside the region to begin manufacturing there. It seems likely that it will be equally successful in protecting its member countries from outside competition. The United States is already reacting; the trade agreement with Canada actually preceded implementation of the EEC tariff reductions. The administration has obtained fast-track authority to negotiate a similar treaty with Mexico; much of North America will trade under regional protection for most of the decade. Furthermore, the administration has floated Latin American trade initiatives, a beginning in the process of involving the whole hemisphere.

The 1990s will therefore see the United States as a strong competitor for much of the business that would previously have gone offshore. Stable wage rates will allow buyers to take advantage of close communications, a growing awareness of the quality responsibilities of suppliers, low freight costs, and no duty or clearance costs. In the following illustration, the XYZ Company compares the U.S. and offshore costs for the same product.

> XYZ Company sells about 10,000 Widgets per month. It has been buying them from a U.S. manufacturer for several years and pays $14.50 each, ex works, 2% 10, net 30. Originally, XYZ negotiated an annual agreement for its requirements and placed orders 90 days in advance. Under the agreement both XYZ and the manufacturer could cancel the agreement with 90 days notice. Subsequent purchases have not been under a formal agreement, but both XYZ and the manufacturer continue to operate as if the original agreement were in effect. The relationship is considered a good one by both parties; XYZ places orders fairly regularly, the manufacturer is responsive to requests to reschedule, in or out, as requested by XYZ. The manufacturer has paid freight both ways to correct defective shipments and done its best to help XYZ recover from the delays caused by the problems.

The business has continued to grow and XYZ has requested quotes from the current vendor and several other firms for next year's requirements. An old school chum of XYZ's president, who brokers for several Far Eastern manufacturers, asked to bid on the business. He returns the following quotation:

DESCRIPTION	QUANTITY	PRICE	
Widgets	25,000	$12.00	FOB Far East
	50,000	$11.00	
	100,000	$10.00	

DELIVERY: 60 days ARO
TERMS: Irrevocable L/C at sight.

The president who, naturally, has received a copy of the quote, wants to realize the savings immediately. He saw the $10 figure, multiplied the $4.50 price reduction times the 120,000 units XYZ Company sells each year, and implies that Purchasing has been wasting $540,000 each year. Reminded that import duty and a few other costs of doing business abroad might affect the price, he asks for details of the savings that will result from moving offshore.

THE PRESIDENT'S WORKSHEET

WIDGET PRICING	OFFSHORE	U.S.A
Vendor's quote:	$10.00	$14.50
SAVINGS PER UNIT		$ 4.50
ANNUAL SAVINGS on 120,000 UNITS		$540,000.00

XYZ's customs broker determines that the duty on a Widget will be 5 percent plus a merchandise processing fee of 0.17 percent. The broker quotes a fee of $125 per entry. In addition, he will charge a $20 messenger fee and $10 for postage, telex, and other communications charges. XYZ plans to buy 10,000 units per month and have one delivery per month.

PURCHASING WORKSHEET (Revision 1)

WIDGET PRICING	OFFSHORE	U.S.A.
Vendor's quote:	$10.00	$14.50
Duty at 5% ad valorem	.50	nil
Customs processing fee	.017	nil

Broker's fees of $125 per entry	.013	nil
Messenger and postage fees	.003	nil
	$10.533	$14.50

SAVINGS PER UNIT $ 3.967
ANNUAL SAVINGS on 120,000 UNITS $476,040.

Because of the volumes XYZ Company will be shipping, the freight forwarder offers a rate of $150 per 1000kg or cubic meter by sea and $2 per kilogram by air.

A Widget, fully packaged, weighs 2.2 lbs. 100 of them, prepared for shipment, occupy 10 cubic feet, or 1 meter. It therefore will cost $1.50 each to ship by sea and $2.00 by air. Shipments will be consolidated with other customers' shipments. Even if XYZ requests 10,000 at a time, the freight will not fill a sea container.

The forwarder agrees to effect delivery from either the sea terminal or the airport for $25 per hundredweight. XYZ has been paying $30 per hundredweight for delivery from the U.S. manufacturer.

PURCHASING WORKSHEET (Revision 2)

WIDGET PRICING	OFFSHORE	U.S.A.
Vendor's quote:	$10.00	$14.50
Duty at 5% ad valorem	.50	nil
Customs processing fee	.017	nil
Broker's fees of $125 per entry	.013	nil
Messenger and postage fees	.003	nil
Seafreight at $150.00 W/M	1.50	nil
Inland Freight	.55	.66
	$12.583	$15.16

SAVINGS PER UNIT $ 2.577
ANNUAL SAVINGS on 120,000 UNITS $309,240.

XYZ Company's business is healthy and the firm has a $1-million line of credit with the bank. Nevertheless, its finance vice-president won't consider exposing $1.2 million in an L/C for an unproven vendor. He does agree to funding a letter for three months. Moreover, he plans to borrow from the bank to fund the letter.

The company can borrow at the prime rate plus 2 percent and estimates its interest rate will be 10 percent. Its deposits earn money-market rates, about 6 percent. In other words, it will cost 4 percent to fund an L/C by borrowing.

The bank will charge $250 to open the L/C and $50 for a full transmission to the supplier's bank. Since this will be the first order, to avoid any surprises, a full letter will be transmitted.

The supplier quoted delivery 60 days after receipt of order. This means that a letter of credit must be funded about 65 days before the first shipment, the additional five days to permit the issuing (XYZ's) bank to prepare and communicate the letter to the advising (supplier's) bank. The L/C expiration date will be set 15 days after shipment to give the supplier time to collect and present the documents to his bank for payment. In all, the L/C may be open 80 days before the first payment is made, 110 days before the second payment, and 140 days before the third. All this time, XYZ Company will be paying 4 percent interest on the unpaid balance.

Would it be cheaper to open three letters of credit? The finance department prepares the following analysis and plans to issue three separate letters of credit.

ANALYSIS: Single Letter of Credit
Three Shipments of 10,000 units at $12.00 unit

Shipment #1
$120,000 at 4% interest for 80 days	$1,052.05
Letter of credit charge	250.00
Full text transmission	50.00

Shipment #2
$120,000 at 4% interest for 110 days	$1,446.58

Shipment #3
$120,000 at 4% interest for 140 days	$1,841.09
TOTAL	$4,639.72
Cost per Widget	.155

ANALYSIS: Three Letters of Credit
Three Shipments of 10,000 units at $12.00 unit

Shipment #1
$120,000 at 4% interest for 80 days	$1,052.05
Letter of credit charge	250.00
Full text transmission	50.00

Shipment #2
$120,000 at 4% interest for 80 days	$1,052.05
Letter of credit charge	250.00
Telex notification	25.00

Shipment #3
$120,000 at 4% interest for 80 days	$1,052.05

Letter of credit charge	250.00
Telex notification	25.00
TOTAL	$4,006.15
Cost per Widget	.134

XYZ Company will own the inventory as soon as it is on board in the Far East. Since shipments from the U.S. manufacturer normally take only two or three days to arrive, buying offshore will create a large in-transit inventory. The cost of carrying this inventory will be a cost of doing business offshore.

Each sea shipment is a 19-day crossing, plus 1 day spent between the vendor's plant and the broker, one day for the broker to consolidate, plus an average of four days before loading. The average 4 days to load includes both the shipping line's requirement for containers to be ready on the dock 48 hours before sailing and an extra 2 days because the line the broker uses sails only once a week. On the average the goods are 6 days in break-bulk and customs. Domestic transit adds another 2 days. Total: 33 days.

The worksheet will include the letter of credit cost and 30 days interest on each monthly shipment; $120,000 at 10% for 30 days is $1000, or $.10 per Widget. The price and duty assumptions change to reflect the higher price of buying fewer units:

PURCHASING WORKSHEET (Revision 3)

WIDGET PRICING	OFFSHORE	U.S.A.
Vendor's quote:	$12.00	$14.50
Duty at 5% ad valorem	.60	nil
Customs processing fee	.02	nil
Broker's fees of $125 per entry	.013	nil
Messenger and postage fees	.003	nil
Seafreight at $150.00 W/M	1.50	nil
Inland freight	.55	.66
Letter of credit cost	.134	nil
Cost of money, inventory in transit	.10	nil
	$14.92	$15.16
SAVINGS PER UNIT		$ 0.24
ANNUAL SAVINGS on 120,000 UNITS	$28,800.	

In a review of the operational issues involved with developing a new source, the vice-president of manufacturing indicates he will not be comfortable switching to a new supplier without an assessment of his capabilities. He proposes sending one of his manufacturing engineers and the quality assurance manager for a week's visit. XYZ Company estimates that at least four people will spend at least 10 days each with the new supplier during the first year. These include a purchasing agent during the negotiations, a senior executive when the agreement is signed, and the quality manager and the manufacturing engineer. Round-trip air fares of $1,500 per person, plus $150 per day for meals and a hotel, add $.10 for travel and living expenses.

The materials manager, concerned about a shaky startup, proposes that, rather than sending the old tools from the U.S. manufacturer, new tools should be made in the Far East. He argues that, should the program fail, orders could then be placed on the U.S. manufacturer. Besides, he says, at volume prices of $10 a Widget, new tools would pay for themselves in a couple of years. The old tools cost about $60,000 including everything needed to manufacture, assemble, and test Widgets, and all the packaging needed to ship and display them. Amortizing the tooling over two years adds $.25 per Widget. The cost of tooling provided for product imported into the United States is dutiable, adding another $.013 per Widget, or 5 percent of the tool amortization.

The quality assurance manager asks how defective product will be handled, especially as XYZ will be paying up-front with an L/C. The materials manager asks whether any verification will be made of the quantities shipped, as only the supplier's commercial invoice will be presented to the bank. There is a quality service company in the supplier's city who will inspect the Widgets at the supplier's before they are to be shipped for a $150 fee plus $20 per hour. The quality manager estimates that it would take a full day to inspect an AQL sample of 5,000 Widgets. Two inspections a month will cost $640, adding $.064 per Widget. The letter of credit will require a source inspection certificate.

PURCHASING WORKSHEET (Revision 4)

WIDGET PRICING	OFFSHORE	U.S.A.
Vendor's quote:	$12.00	$14.50
Duty at 5% ad valorem	.60	nil
Customs processing fee	.02	nil
Broker's fees of $125 per entry	.013	nil
Messenger and postage fees	.003	nil
Seafreight at $150.00 W/M	1.50	nil
Inland freight	.55	.66
Letter of credit cost	.134	nil
Cost of money, inventory in transit	.10	nil

Duplicate tool amortization	.25	nil
Dutiable assists	.013	nil
Travel and communications	.10	nil
Source inspection	.064	nil
	$15.347	$15.16
SAVINGS PER UNIT	(loss	$ .187)
ANNUAL SAVINGS on 120,000 UNITS	(loss	$22,440.)

The president still feels that the offshore option offers a greater savings to XYZ Company. He suspects his old school chum included at least a 15-percent commission for himself and suggests the purchase price could be reduced by "at least $.50." He suggests negotiating an annual agreement, placing 25,000 unit orders for each of the next two quarters and, thereafter, for six months at a time. These two changes reduce the average purchase price assumption to $11.00.

He is willing to overrule the company's finance vice-president and fund the letters of credit through the bank line. Since monthly L/Cs are reflected in the worksheet, he does not feel the $120,000 exposure is too great. The L/C interest costs are eliminated.

PURCHASING WORKSHEET (Final)

WIDGET PRICING	OFFSHORE	U.S.A.
Vendor's quote:	$11.00	$14.50
Duty at 5% ad valorem	.55	nil
Customs processing fee	.019	nil
Broker's fees of $125 per entry	.013	nil
Messenger and postage fees	.003	nil
Seafreight at $150.00 W/M	1.50	nil
Inland freight	.55	.66
Letter of credit cost	.014	nil
Cost of money, inventory in transit	.10	nil
Duplicate tool amortization	.25	nil
Dutiable assists	.013	nil
Travel and communications	.10	nil
	$14.197	$15.16
SAVINGS PER UNIT		$ 1.048
ANNUAL SAVINGS on 120,000 UNITS		$125,760.

XYZ Company's worksheets show a common discovery: The actual costs of doing business offshore are very often much greater than anticipated. We showed the XYZ Company in a process of identifying the added costs before an order was placed. Unfortunately, many companies learn of them when the invoices start coming in.

The "final" worksheet is a little flourish to illustrate another, all too common, mistake. Any analysis of this kind can be made to look good. The new assumptions provided by the president of XYZ now support going offshore. Whether the new assumptions are valid, or some other important ones are missing, won't be known until the XYZ Company's invoices start arriving.

THE U.S. MANUFACTURER

The other point we want to make with the XYZ case is that few companies recognize cost-reduction opportunities at their U.S. suppliers. Review the advantages being given the offshore supplier in the preceding case:

1. The U.S. manufacturer has not had an annual agreement since the first year. Operating "as if" an agreement were in place does not provide him the same security to place volume orders for material, or longer contract with his own subcontractors.

   The offshore supplier will start with an annual agreement.

2. The U.S. manufacturer receives "fairly regular" orders and is appreciated for his flexibility in rescheduling orders. He is actually absorbing some of XYZ Company's cost of money when he delays a shipment and paying premiums or overtime when he ships earlier than originally requested.

   The offshore supplier has a firm commitment and, once the L/C is issued, is under no pressure or obligation to ship earlier or delay shipment.

3. The XYZ Company buys from the U.S. manufacturer on open account and, although XYZ is a healthy company, the manufacturer has some credit risk.

   The L/C ensures the offshore supplier has no credit risk.

4. The U.S. manufacturer offers 30-day terms.

The offshore supplier can draw down the L/C as soon as the Widgets are on board.

This differential could have been quantified in our worksheets. We did not include it to emphasize that open account payment is so common in the United States that its value is often not appreciated. The worksheet would reflect the cost of money over 30 days, or the 2-percent prompt pay reduction. It would not quantify the value to small companies who hold checks because of a tight cash situation, or chronically finance their business on 50- or 60-day payables.

5. If the XYZ Company is like most U.S. companies, nobody has visited the U.S. manufacturer since the first order was placed, if then.

   XYZ plans to support the offshore supplier with 40 work days of purchasing, quality, manufacturing engineering, and executive personnel to resolve any purchasing, process, product, or quality questions that may arise.

6. Inbound freight costs from the U.S. manufacturer have probably not been renegotiated for years.

   The freight estimates for the offshore alternative reflect current bids, which recognize the volume, and value, of the XYZ account.

7. The U.S. manufacturer has paid freight both ways to correct defective shipments and done his best to help XYZ recover from the delays caused by the problems.

   Source inspection is planned for the offshore manufacturer. Any defective lots will be identified at his plant, where corrective action can take place immediately without extraordinary expense.

8. Widgets from the U.S. manufacturer are two days away. Even during shortage situations, freight delay is negligible compared to production time.

   The worksheets do not reflect the impact of any shipments that may need to be expedited. Airfreight will add

$.50 per Widget to the cost, not including possible costs for customs overtime or special deliveries from the freight forwarder.

The XYZ Company's worksheets do not give the U.S. manufacturer a level playing field. The fault does not lie with any foreign government but with the XYZ Company. Moreover, no recognition is given the ardor with which a new supplier goes after new business, or the efforts a current supplier would give to keep an old customer.

Our experience indicates that U.S. manufacturers of a wide range of products, given the same conditions offered an offshore supplier and the knowledge that the competition will be intense, can often equal or better the prices and terms available offshore. During the 1990s we expect that U.S. manufacturers will become even more competitive. This is certainly not true of everything, especially products that have a high unskilled or semiskilled labor content. It is common enough that professional buyers will do all they can to keep a current supplier informed as to their competitive position.

Last, there are many intangibles that may favor doing business in the United States, all other factors being equal. Of these, communication is clearly the most important. Business can generally be conducted without the impediment of different time zones. Holidays are almost uniform in the United States whereas different holidays worldwide are no small inconvenience buying offshore. Nuance in language is an infrequent cause of misunderstanding and no effort is necessary for translation. Business culture and commercial law are so uniform nationwide that few misunderstandings arise because of them. Local business practices must be learned offshore. In the United States, much discussion and negotiation is avoided because common practice is mutually understood.

There is really no such thing as an offshore buyer, an expression used throughout this book; there are only offshore sources. Good buyers will continually reassess the market for products, and any who fail to continually reassess the United States as an option aren't doing the job.

REFERENCES

CHAPTER 1

Gill, Stephen and David Law. *Global Political Economy*. Baltimore, MD: Johns Hopkins University Press, 1988. International policy questions examined, especially with regard to economic, ecological, and national security issues.

Librenz, Marilyn L. *Transfer of Technology*. New York: Praeger, 1982. Using actual case histories, the author has abstracted a list of factors to consider in a technology transfer to a foreign country.

Rogowski, Ronald. *Commerce and Coalition: How Trade Affects Domestic Political Alignments*. Princeton, NJ: Princeton University Press, 1989. The author suggests that trade issues directly affect U.S. political coalitions, examining the interplay between them.

Porter, Michael. *The Comparative Advantage of Nations and Their Firms*. New York: The Free Press, 1990. Porter has written several books on competition, this one dealing with national impacts on the firm's competitiveness.

Rostow, W. W. *The Process of Economic Growth*. New York: W. W. Norton, 1962. An analysis of international growth and some economic theories about the stages of growth that a developing country goes through.

Preeg, Ernest, ed. *Hard Bargaining Ahead: U.S. Trade Policy and Developing Countries*. Washington, D.C.: Overseas Development Council, 1985. A collection of articles to note the issues that the United States faces in trade policy negotiations.

CHAPTER 2

Muller, Georg. *Comparative World Data*. Baltimore MD: Johns Hopkins University Press, 1988.

Index to International Statistics; Government Statistics Summary Book. Bethesda, MD: Congressional Information Service, 1989. Statistics indexed by subject, country name, geographic region. Details financial and economic basic statistics. For example: Thailand: major economic indicators—employment, unemployment, hours wages and/or price index, source: IMF Monthly Report. Some sources for data are available for further reference in a library (e.g., UNESCO data) whereas other sources must be purchased.

European Marketing Data and Statistics. London: Euromonitor Publications LTD, 1984.

Asia 1990. Hong Kong: Review Publishing Co., 1990. Regional demographic, production, public sector expenditure, and foreign trade data for 30 countries throughout Asia.

China Statistical Abstract. New York: Praeger, 1990. Abstracted from the State Statistical Bureau of the People's Republic of China.

Japan Economic Almanac. Tokyo: Japan Economic Journal, 1990. Includes economic forecasts and news.

Ryans, Cynthia C. *International Business Reference Sources*. Lexington, MA: D. C. Heath, 1984. A directory of books and directories of international business organizations and other business data sources.

Kurian, George Thomas. *Sourcebook of Global Statistics*. New York: Facts on File, 1985. Tells where the statistics are: what book, how to order, whether on disk, etc.

How to Find Information About Companies. Washington, D.C.: Washington Researchers, latest edition.

Kruzas, Anthony T. and Robert C. Thomas. *Business Organizations and Agencies Directory*. Detroit, MI: Gale Research, 1980. A worldwide guide to that in the title, plus a lot more.

American Export Register, formerly *American Register of Exporters and Importers*. New York: Thomas International, 1990.

World Guide to Trade Associations. Munich: K. G. Saur, 1985.

Business Directory of Hong Kong. Hong Kong: Current Publications LTD, 1983.

Buy From India. Bombay: Buy From India Publishers, 1988. A directory of Indian exporters.

How to Find Information About Japanese Companies and Industries. Washington, D.C.: Washington Researchers LTD, 1984.

International Marketing Handbook. Detroit, MI: Gale Research Company, 1985 or latest. Detailed marketing profiles for 142 nations with fundamental data for developing and export marketing effort or importing to the United States.

CHAPTER 3

Axtell, Roger E. *Do's and Taboos Around the World.* New York: John Wiley & Sons, 1990.

Axtell, Roger E. *Do's and Taboos of Hosting International Visitors.* New York: John Wiley & Sons, 1990.

Culturegrams from the David M. Kennedy Center for International Studies, Brigham Young University, Provo, Utah 84602.

Zimmerman, Mark. *How to do Business With the Japanese.* New York: Random House, 1985.

CHAPTER 4

Moran, Robert T. *Getting Your Yen's Worth: How to Negotiate.* Houston, TX: Gulf Publishing, 1987.

Win-win Negotiating: Turning Conflict into Negotiation. New York: John Wiley & Sons, 1985.

Axtell, Roger E. *Do's and Taboos of International Trade.* New York: John Wiley & Sons, 1989.

CHAPTER 5

U.S. Export Administration Regulations. U.S. Department of Commerce, International Trade Administration. Latest edition: January 1990. A subscription service is available for Export Administration Bulletins, which append, amend, and supplement each edition. Available from the Superintendent of Documents, Washington, D.C. 20402.

MacKenzie, Charles H. C.; Michael E. Power; and Ted. L. Dorman. *Shipping Conferences.* Lexington, MA: D. C. Heath, 1985. A bibli-

ography of books and other references concerning shipping conferences, how they work, etc.

Johnson, Thomas E. *Export-Import Procedures and Documents*. New
York: American Management Association, 1991.

Policiano, Dominic J. *Letter of Credit Guidebook*. New York: Executive
Education Press, 1983. The bank "insider" we use to confirm our
suspicions about L/Cs states that this is the definitive source. We
left out "Red clause" letters as too risky (our insider won't even issue
them, preferring transferable ones) but Policiano explains them: If
you need to advance payment to your supplier for materials or whatever, a Red Clause might be used. Given the Soviets' abuse of L/Cs
in the past we expect they will opt for these as often as possible,
even if the pun no longer applies.

Woollam, W. G. *Shipping Terms and Abbreviations*. Cambridge, MA:
Cornell Maritime Press, Inc., 1963.

CHAPTER 6

World Currency Yearbook. Brooklyn, NY: International Currency Analysis, Inc., latest edition. A thorough discussion of currency exchange
rates and related information. For example, shows official versus
unofficial range of exchange for affected currencies versus the US$,
notes currencies pegged directly to the US$ and currencies pegged
to a "basket" of currencies; reports black market premiums or discounts for the US$ (USSR ruble was 512% in 1986).

Operating in a Floating Rate World. New York: Business International
Corporation, 1976. Deals with problems of floating exchange rates.

Steinberg, Eleanor B. and Joseph A. Yager. *New Means of Financing
International Needs*. Washington, D.C.: Brookings Institution, 1978.
A dry look at the practices and economics of international finance
and ideas for improvement.

Kingman-Brundage, Jane and Susan A. Schulz. *Fundamentals of Trade
Finance*. New York: John Wiley & Sons, 1986. The ins and outs of
import-export financing.

Fildes, Robert. *World Index of Economic Forecasts*. New York: Stockton
Press, 1988. Lists organizations that publish forecasts of economic
activity. Gives the name, address, telephone number, and contact
name of each organization, a short description of the subject area(s)
of the forecast, and the price to subscribe.

CHAPTER 7

Crosby, Philip B. *Quality Is Free: The Art of Making Quality Certain.* New York: McGraw-Hill, 1979.

Deming, W. E. *Quality, Production and Competitive Position.* Cambridge, MA: Center for Advanced Engineering, Massachussetts Institute of Technology, 1982.

Feigenbaum, Armand V. *Total Quality Control.* New York: McGraw-Hill, 1983.

Ouchi, William G. *Theory Z: How American Business Can Meet the Japanese Challenge.* Reading, MA: Addison-Wesley, 1981.

Taguchi, Genichi. *Introduction to Quality Engineering: Designing Quality into Products and Processes.* White Plains, NY: Quality Resources Div. of Kraus Organization, 1986.

INDEX

A

Accounts, Open
  and improving payment sched-
    ules, 180–81
  as terms of payment, 177–78
Agendas
  as negotiating tactic, 129
Agents, 54–55
Arbitrage, 169–70
Argentina, 34–35
  See also Latin America
ASEAN (Association of South East-
    ern Asian Nations), 20
Asia
  information on, 5
  Japan compared to other countries
    in, 20–21
  as procurement source, 18–21
  southern countries compared to
    other nations, 21
  See also specific countries
Asian *Wall Street Journal*, 5
Association of South Eastern Asian
    Nations (ASEAN), 20
Australia
  as procurement source, 24–25
  profile of, 32–33

B

Batam, 20
Bond, Customs, 153–54

Brazil, 34–35, 205
  See also Latin America
Brokers, 53, 58
Bulgaria
  development in, 16
  profile of, 36–37
  See also Eastern Europe
Bush, George, 17, 28
Business Cards, 89–91, 91–92
Business Trips
  dining on, 94–97
  entertainment while on, 93–100
  etiquette for, 85–105
  nightlife on, 97–99
  shopping during, 104–5
  women and, 87–88

C

Canada, 38
Captive Supplier, 59, 65
Carriage Paid To (CPT), 146
CFR (Cost and Freight), 144
Charges, Shipping, 157–58
Checklists
  for business trips, 105
  for finding quality suppliers,
    73–75
  for judging procurement sources,
    29–30
  for managing payments, 183–84
  for managing suppliers, 210
  for negotiations, 136–37

About APICS

APICS, the educational society for resource management, offers the resources professionals need to succeed in the manufacturing community. With more than 35 years of experience, 70,000 members, and 260 local chapters, APICS is recognized worldwide for setting the standards for professional education. The society offers a full range of courses, conferences, educational programs, certification processes, and materials developed under the direction of industry experts.

APICS offers everything members need to enhance their careers and increase their professional value. Benefits include:

- Two internationally recognized educational certification processes—Certified in Production and Inventory Management (CPIM) and Certified in Integrated Resource Management (CIRM), which provide immediate recognition in the field and enhance members' work-related knowledge and skills. The CPIM process focuses on depth of knowledge in the core areas of production and inventory management, while the CIRM process supplies a breadth of knowledge in 13 functional areas of the business enterprise.
- The APICS Educational Materials Catalog—a handy collection of courses, proceedings, reprints, training materials, videos, software, and books written by industry experts...many of which are available to members at substantial discounts.
- *APICS The Performance Advantage*—a monthly magazine that focuses on improving competitiveness, quality, and productivity.
- Specific industry groups (SIGs)—suborganizations that develop educational programs, offer accompanying materials, and provide valuable networking opportunities.
- A multitude of educational workshops, employment referral, insurance, a retirement plan, and more.

To join APICS, or for complete information on the many benefits and services of APICS membership, **call 1-800-444-2742** or **703-237-8344**. Use extension 297.